A FORGE OF
FREEDOM BOOK

The Thirteen Colonies
~1763~

THE
NEW HAMPSHIRE
COLONY

by
Daniel H. Giffen

CROWELL-COLLIER PRESS
Collier-Macmillan Limited, London

Library of Congress Catalog Card Number: 76–93178

The Macmillan Company
Collier-Macmillan Canada Ltd., Toronto, Ontario
Printed in the United States of America

FIRST PRINTING

PICTURE CREDITS

Culver Pictures, Inc., 20, 57, 79; New Hampshire Historical Society, 4, 8, 11, 14, 22, 27, 39, 47, 48; New Hampshire Historical Society (photographs by Bill Finney), 12, 17, 31, 36, 59, 62, 80, 85, 88.

JACKET ILLUSTRATION: *The construction of a mast ship*

For Jane, Sarah and Thomas

Contents

THE
NEW HAMPSHIRE
COLONY

1

The Early Explorers

In the village of North Salem, New Hampshire, lie the ruins of some twenty-two stone huts. In the center of the area is a huge, four-and-a-half-ton granite slab, resting horizontally on crude logs. Cut along the top rim of the slab is an inch-deep groove, from which liquid can drain into a small trough. This giant slab is all that remains of what probably was once an ancient religious altar.

In other parts of the ruins, there are ramps, walks, squares and connecting stone cells, giving the impression that an active community once thrived there.

Archaeologists have long been fascinated by this primitive village, and for excellent reason. No one knows for certain how it got there, who built the houses or when and how they were constructed.

Some scholars have tried to prove that the settlement was either Irish or Norse and that it was created around the year 1000 A.D. Ancient stories do relate that both Irish and

Viking ships once landed in New England, probably during the eleventh and twelfth centuries, but no one can prove this for sure.

Perhaps through further study and investigation the North Salem ruins will unlock the secret of the first settlement in New Hampshire. Until that secret is unlocked, though, we must begin to trace New Hampshire's history from a much later date—around the time of Columbus.

Not long after the New World was discovered, many European rulers began sending voyagers westward to seek out its riches and natural treasures. Within a short time, explorers were enthusiastically reporting that off the coast of northern New England lay some of the richest and most fertile fishing areas they had ever seen.

As word of this find spread during the sixteenth century, more and more ships began heading for the New England coast. Many probably touched land at New Hampshire, but as far as we know, most of these early sailors just hauled in large catches of fish and then returned home. Although the New Hampshire coast was certainly becoming more and more familiar to European sailors, it was still to be some time before anyone considered actually living there.

Ventures into the interior of New England became more frequent after 1600. A number of joint-stock companies were formed under the charter of the English king, for the purpose of financing and carrying out exploration. It was hoped that the discovery of more valuable treasures than fish would bring quick profits to the numerous stockholders as well as to the king himself.

In 1603, the mayor, the alderman and a number of merchants from the rich English city of Bristol fitted out a small expedition under the leadership of a man named Martin Pring. Pring became the first explorer to leave behind a written record of his trip to New Hampshire, even though the purpose of his expedition was the study of the northern parts of "Virginia."

With twenty-nine other men, Pring crossed the Atlantic in a fifty-ton ship called the *Speedwell*. Accompanying him was a twenty-six-ton bark, the *Discoverer,* which carried an additional thirteen men. They landed near the entrance of Penobscot Bay and then made their way to the Piscataqua River, which Pring called "the westernmost and best river." He and his men explored it ten miles into the interior.

Later, in the month of June, Pring and his two ships arrived near the present town of Portsmouth and set anchor in the lower harbor. The *Discoverer,* not much larger than a sloop, was soon rowed upstream for further exploration. Occasionally the crew made short side trips inland through vast forests populated by wild animals and, in his record, Pring commented on the "goodly groves and woods."

Pring's party had hoped to see some Indians along the river. The men were in for a disappointment, though, because June was the season when fish were more plentiful farther inland in smaller bodies of water, and the Indians had left the riverside in search of the best possible catch.

The absence of Indians was not Pring's only disappointment. One of the "riches" he was looking for was the sassafras tree. In those days, sassafras bark was thought to contain the "elixir of life," and had Pring been able to bring some home he would have been a very wealthy man indeed. Having continued up the river as far as Great Bay, and failing to find any sign of the tree, Pring's party altered course and headed south.

Just about the same time, explorers from other countries were visiting the New Hampshire coast. The French expedition of Samuel de Champlain, for instance, cruised along New Hampshire during the summer of 1605 and again in

1606. During his 1605 visit, Champlain probably touched on a point of land, a spot that later became famous as Pannaway, the first permanent settlement in New Hampshire.

It is said that Champlain met a small party of Indians there and gave them presents of knives and small tools. In exchange, the Indians drew Champlain a charcoal sketch of the coastline, as far as they knew it. This sketch turned out to be extremely valuable, for it showed the entrance to the Merrimack River, which no white man had ever heard of before.

In 1614, during his exploration of "The Virginia Coast," another famous explorer, Captain John Smith, visited New Hampshire. With two ships, Smith arrived at Monhegan Island, off the coast of Maine. He and his men fished and studied the coastline from Penobscot Bay to Cape Cod, Massachusetts. Captain Smith also touched upon the Isles of Shoals, already famous for the great schools of fish in their waters. He named the area Smith's Isles. Smith drew the first map of the coast to be printed, and this map, along with his enthusiastic tales of the New World, encouraged

Captain John Smith explored the coast of New Hampshire in 1614

for the drying of fish. The knoll on which these flakes were built still bears the name of Flake Hill.

During the early days of the plantation, the settlers suffered many hardships, and a good number of the men were stricken by fatal diseases. The first graveyard, with moss-covered stones at the head and foot of each grave, may still be seen near the site of the Pannaway House.

The plantation was visited by many now famous settlers from Plymouth Colony in neighboring Massachusetts. Miles Standish is said to have come to Pannaway early in 1623 on his way home from a journey northward. Another important visitor was Christopher Levett, who had come to New England in the spring of 1624 to establish a coastal city to be named York, after a British city of the same name.

While Levett was visiting Pannaway, Governor Robert Gorges, son of Sir Ferdinando, arrived with a commission appointing himself lieutenant general and governor of New England, and naming Levett as a member of the governor's council. So it was at Pannaway that Levett was installed in his high office, in a ceremony performed by Governor Gorges and three other members of his council.

Pannaway Plantation remained in the care of David Thomson and his partners for about seven years, but it was abandoned before 1630. Even though Pannaway Plantation was short-lived, it was of considerable importance to the development of the New Hampshire colony. It was the first of a series of small, isolated settlements that began dotting the necks and points of the Great Bay during the first half of the seventeenth century. Once these outposts were established, it was possible for settlers to begin penetrating to the inland portion of the province.

Most early voyagers to the coast of New Hampshire actually had little interest in the far-reaching territory beyond the first falls of the Piscataqua River. They were still mainly interested in catching and drying the cod fish that were so abundant in the deep waters off Little Harbor and around the Isles of Shoals. If it had not been for this great wealth in fishing, the settlement of this portion of New England might have been delayed almost a century. Certainly New Hampshire's rocky coastline, sandy fields and scrub timber offered little for the farmer. However, the good fishing—particularly for cod—continually drew settlers to New Hampshire.

Eventually towns were chartered, and houses and churches were built. Farms were laid out in the more fertile portions of the territory, and New Hampshire settled down to become an important member of the original English colonies on the North American continent. Before it was possible for colonists to create a stable and permanent province, though, there were many obstacles to overcome.

An early New Hampshire home

2

Getting Acquainted
with the Indians

Generally speaking, the Indians of New Hampshire were a peaceful people. They numbered only about four thousand at the time of the early explorers, and they lived in various small villages scattered throughout the colony.

In the eastern areas, for instance, lived the Ossipees, the Pequawkets and several other tribes, who made up a large group known as the Abenaki tribes. Farther inland lived the Pennacook confederacy of tribes, which included the Pennacooks, who inhabited the Merrimack Valley near Concord, and the Piscataquas, who lived at the present site of Dover. Despite this great variety of tribal names, nearly all of the New Hampshire Indians were members of the same nation—the Algonquins.

Had Martin Pring, John Smith or any of the other early explorers happened to stumble upon a typical Indian village, they would have been quite surprised at how small it was. Probably none of the Indian villages contained more than two hundred people, and many contained less than fifty.

New Hampshire Indians spent much of their time hunting, fishing, farming small fields of land and trapping animals for their pelts. Some of these pelts were kept and fashioned into clothing and moccasins, while others were used for trade with neighboring tribes. Around the village, Indian women planted and tended to small fields of maize, pumpkins and other vegetables. These activities, as well as a small amount of trade in maple products with other Algonquin tribes, formed the basis of the New Hampshire Indian economy.

The Indians, on the whole, were a very mobile people, and they often traveled about within a sizeable area. Sometimes, in fact, entire villages were moved from one part of New Hampshire to another.

Transportation presented little problem. The Indians had become experts in the art of making snowshoes from saplings and bands of twisted shoots and straw, and these served very well for overland travel during the winter season.

Taking advantage of the many natural waterways in the area, the Indians had also become experts at constructing both birchbark and dugout canoes, and these were used for traveling on the Merrimack and Connecticut rivers, as well as on New Hampshire's numerous lakes.

At the time of his first journey to the mouth of the Piscataqua River, Captain John Smith observed that the customs and language of the Indians of the Great Bay area were strikingly similar to those of the Indians who lived both to the east and west of them. The reason for this is simple. Although there were many separate tribes living in the area, they were all united under one ruler, a man called Bashaba, who lived in Penobscot (now in the state of Maine).

Indians' recreation sometimes included playing ball on the ice

Shortly after Smith's venture into the Piscataqua region in the summer of 1614, peace was shattered when the Pequawket Nation was invaded by the Tarateens, a tribe who lived farther to the east. The Tarateens surprised and killed Bashaba, slew many men of his tribe and carried off the women. The loss of Bashaba soon created civil war among the individual tribal chiefs, who disagreed about who should take Bashaba's place. By the end of 1614, many of the Pequawkets had been killed, and much of their lands and many of their villages were ruined.

Just how bad things were can be seen from a report by Sir Richard Hawkins, who visited the area when the war was still at its height in 1615. "The war," he wrote, "was succeeded by a pestilence which carried off the Indians in such numbers that the living were unable to bury their dead and their bones remained at the places of their habitations for several years."

At the same time, though, Sir Ferdinando Gorges had sent a party of men, led by Richard Vines, to winter among the Indians in the Great Bay area. Vines and his men reported a completely different kind of experience. They lived as the Indians did, ate their food and even shared their huts, "not so much as feeling their heads to ache the whole time."

Fortunately for the Indians, civil conflicts, such as the Pequawket Wars, were rare. By the middle of the seventeenth century, what remained of the Pequawket tribes had become reunited with the tribes of the Pawtucket and Winnipesaukee areas. Their new leader was the great Sachem (Algonquin for "chief") Passaconaway, the sagamore of the Pennacooks.

Passaconaway was said to excel the other sachems, not only in his physical skills but in his talents as a sorcerer as well. His reputation had spread among all the neighboring tribes, and his influence was great. The Indians believed

Passaconaway, the Indian chieftain and wizard

that "it was in his power to make water run, and trees dance, and to change himself into a flame." It was also said that in the winter time he changed dry leaves to green, and that he was able to create a living snake from the dried skin of a dead one.

Toward the end of his reign in 1660, Passaconaway gave a great feast and invited a number of the Englishmen who were in the area at the time. During the festivities, elderly tribesmen made speeches and sang songs in which they explained the history of the various tribes. Passaconaway, realizing the need for cooperation with the English colonists, made a farewell speech to his people, in which he warned them of the dangers of quarreling with their English neighbors. He told his people that, though they might do harm to the English, in the long run such quarrels would prove to be a means for their own destruction. He is also said to have told his followers that, though he had been a great enemy of the English, and through his magical arts had tried to hinder them from settling in his country, it was outside even his supernatural powers to stop them.

So great was the influence of Passaconaway that, fifteen years later, when war broke out between the Indians and the settlers of the neighboring Plymouth colony, Passaconaway's son and successor, Wonolancet, withdrew from the Pennacook Confederacy and fled with his people into the wilderness.

Not all Indian sachems and their followers, though, were as peaceful as Passaconaway, Wonolancet and the Pennacooks. During the years between 1675 and 1697, isolated settlements throughout the New Hampshire colony were subject to quick, fierce attacks by wandering parties of Indians. These attacks were prompted either by the Indians' desire for the possessions of the settlers or by fear that the Indians' hunting grounds and peaceful valleys would be completely taken over by the white men.

Isolated settlements were subject to quick, fierce attacks by the Indians

The Dustin family attempts to escape from the Indians

Many New Hampshire outposts were taken, and many families were massacred during this period. The most famous woman captured by the Indians in the New Hampshire territory at this time was Hannah Dustin. Hannah and her husband Thomas lived in the town of Haverhill, Massachusetts, with their eight children, including a baby only one week old, and a nurse named Mary Neff. At this time, there were only a few widely scattered houses in Haverhill, and only a small portion of the land was under cultivation. The Indians in the area had been troublesome, and occasional outbreaks of violence had already occurred. In the fall of 1696, many people had been massacred, and the Indians had taken several prisoners across the border into Canada.

Then, on March 15, 1697, Haverhill was attacked without warning by twenty Indians in full warpaint. The Dustin house, on the outskirts of the settlement, was the first to be seized. Mr. Dustin had been working in the fields and had seen the Indians coming in time to run home to his family. He told his older children to hurry to a fort that was located about a mile away, and then went to his wife's bedside to help move her and the newborn child to the same place of safety. The Indians reached the house before Mrs. Dustin could even leave her bed. Agonized over the fate of his seven children, who were on their way to the garrison, Dustin rushed out of the house to follow them, firing at the Indians as he ran.

Luckily, Dustin succeeded in placing his children in the fort, where they were safe. In the meantime, however, his house was burned, and Mrs. Dustin, her baby and Mary Neff, the nurse, were taken captive. Although Mrs. Neff tried to escape with the baby, she was quickly recaptured, and along with Mrs. Dustin, the entire party began a journey toward Canada. Before they got very far, though, the baby began to cry and was immediately killed.

During the next few days, the party traveled over one hundred and fifty miles through New Hampshire toward Canada. Eventually, they arrived at a small island in the Merrimack River near Concord. Camp was made, and the captives were put to work as slaves for an Indian family of two men, three women and seven children. On March 30, a messenger arrived from another Indian encampment and told the group of a plan to torture the two white women. To Mrs. Dustin and her companion, the fear of torture and their longing for their loved ones was maddening.

That night, as the Indians slept soundly around the campfire, Mrs. Dustin decided that it was worth the risk of her life to try to make her escape. With Mrs. Neff and another white captive, a boy named Samuel Leonardson, Hannah Dustin armed herself with her captors' axes, and struck blow upon blow on the heads of the sleeping Indians. Only one squaw and a small child survived. Taking the scalps of ten Indians and a few silver trinkets, Mrs. Dustin and the nurse escaped in one of their captors' canoes, and paddled down the Merrimack River back to Haverhill.

Mrs. Dustin's safe return was not merely rejoiced by her loved ones, who had nearly given her up for dead. She was also publicly honored and amply rewarded for her bravery. The ten scalps were taken to Boston, where a reward of fifty pounds was presented to her by the court. She also was showered with gifts from admirers throughout the colonies, including Colonel Francis Nickerson, the governor of Maryland, who sent her a substantial sum of money.

Adventure stories, such as that of Hannah Dustin's frightening ordeal, naturally had the effect of representing the Indians as a revengeful, treacherous and jealous people, filled with nothing but hatred for white men. At the same time, though, it must be remembered that many Indians were so badly treated by certain settlers that they had just cause for their hostility.

Although many of the settlers purchased their lands from the Indians for fair prices, others used fraudulent methods to cheat the Indians out of their land. This was particularly common in the eastern portions of the state. Although such dealings were outlawed by the government and were punished whenever a complaint was made, the Indians knew only the laws they had always used among themselves. When injury was received, it was never forgotten until revenged.

Unfair land-trading or trespassing were sufficient grounds for a quarrel and kept alive a constant hostility, causing some Indians to take out their grievances on innocent settlers.

A small silver ornament cut from an Indian's clothing by Hannah Dustin on the night she escaped

Goodly Groves
and Early Settlements

The Indians had good reason to be jealous of the white man's sudden claim to their territory. New Hampshire was a land of great natural beauty—the ideal home for small bands of people who lived a simple, outdoor life. There were great stocks of fish and game in the rivers and forests, over a thousand lakes and enough clear meadows to plant small crops of pumpkins and maize.

To the white man, though, coming from the comfortable, well-settled countryside of England, New Hampshire was not so much a beautiful setting for a simple, rugged way of life as it was a land of excitement and mystery. The coastline presented an intriguing and terrifying panorama. The wilderness beyond the shore seemed to promise almost every kind of natural wealth imaginable.

The most adventurous of the early explorers were eager to push quickly into the interior. Early records describe many lakes and rivers extending back to an enormous "great lake," dotted with beautiful islands. One of these explorers, Captain Walter Neale, described the air as "pure and salubrious," and the country as "pleasant, having high hills, full of goodly forests, fair valleys, and fertile plains." He also praised the many fruits of the land—the Indian maize, the grapes, the various nuts, and the fine timber that surrounded the open meadows. He was not the only one to remark about the delicately flavored fish that were so plentiful in the rivers and streams.

It was the mountains that seemed to make the greatest impression on Neale and other early explorers. In 1632, Captain Neale and a few others set out on foot for territory now known as the Lakes Region and the White Mountains. They hoped to establish trade with the Indians and to discover what riches might be hidden in the mountain ranges. During the course of their journey, they came across the "great lake," and climbed the rugged Ossipee Mountain Range. They also traveled inland to the White Mountains, where they discovered the ranges now known by the names of Presidential, Franconia and Sandwich. They described in great romantic style the ridge of mountains extending a hundred leagues (about three hundred miles) "on which snow lieth all year, and inaccessible except by the gullies which the dissolved snow hath made."

Neale and his party had expected to find gold or precious stones among the mountains. They didn't find gold, but they did discover something resembling crystal—deposits of mica—and they named the entire complex of mountain ranges the Crystal Hills.

After climbing the highest peak in the range, now known as Mount Washington, they moved onward in the hope of finding yet another "great lake." Their food and water were soon nearly gone, though, and they were forced to return to Great Bay.

The "great lake" the party discovered was Lake Winni-

*In 1632, Captain Walter Neale and a few others
explored the White Mountains*

pesaukee, the largest in New Hampshire and one of the
largest fresh-water lakes in the United States lying wholly
within the boundaries of one state. Neale and his men
didn't penetrate far enough into the interior to discover the
Merrimack and Connecticut river valleys. Nor did they
explore the mountain ranges thoroughly enough to be
aware of any of the "great notches"—notches formed thou-
sands of years ago, during the great Ice Age, when snow
and glaciers moved slowly across the continent, covering the
mountains.

What the early explorers did see, however, filled them
with wonder, and they returned to England with enthusiastic reports about the New Hampshire interior. The
people who decided to come over to New Hampshire to live,
however, were reluctant to set up their homes in the middle
of the wilderness. In fact, during the first fifty years that
followed David Thomson's original settlement at Panna-

way, only four towns—Portsmouth, Dover, Exeter and
Hampton—were established, and all of them were near
Great Bay.

The first of these towns to be settled was Dover. Dover,
then called Northam, and later Dover Neck were founded
by Edward and William Hilton, two brothers who had been
fishmongers in London. Both Edward and William may
have been members of a group that left Pannaway in 1623
or 1624 and traveled eight miles up the Piscataqua River to
settle the small plantation of Dover Point.

In 1629, after much hard work, Edward Hilton asked
for a patent from the Council for New England. His request
was granted, and the patent he received covered "all that
part of the river Piscataqua called or known by the name
of Hilton's Point, with the south side of said river, up to the
falls of Squamscot, and three miles into the mainland for
breadth." This area included the sites of the present towns
of Dover, Durham, Stratham and parts of Greenland.

The patent, known as the Squamscot Patent, stated that
at his own expense, Hilton had transported men, built
houses and established farms at Hilton's Point, and that he
intended to continue developing his settlement there.
Three men, William Blackstone, William Jeffries and
Thomas Lewis, were given the power to assign pieces of
Hilton's land to the individual settlers.

Under the terms of the Squamscot Patent, two thirds of
the interest in the settlement belonged to a company of
Bristol merchants. These merchants, hoping to develop the
area, tried to convince five hundred people to come to Dover
in the year 1633, and an immigration voyage was arranged
under the leadership of a man named Captain Thomas
Wiggin. Only a small number of families actually made the
trip and claimed land. Most of those who did come were
more interested in trading with the Indians than in anything else. So they took only small plots of land on Dover
Neck, which lies between two branches of the Piscataqua,

and was well situated for trade. Consequently, only a few large tracts of land were developed for farming.

On the highest point of Dover Neck the settlers built a meetinghouse, which they surrounded with embankments, palisades and trenches, so that it could also serve as a fort. William Leveridge, "a worthy and able Puritan minister," was brought over during the first year, but the settlement was too poor to support him, and he moved on to Massachusetts.

The loss of William Leveridge was only the beginning of Dover's troubles, but its settlers worked hard against many odds, and by 1640 the town was both peaceful and prosperous.

At about the same time that Hilton obtained the Squamscot Patent, a new joint-stock company was formed. It was called the Laconia Company, and its most important members were Sir Ferdinando Gorges of the Council for New England and Captain John Mason. Mason was also closely associated with the council and had already had experience in the New World as governor of Newfoundland.

The meetinghouse at Dover Neck also served as a fort

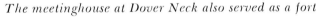

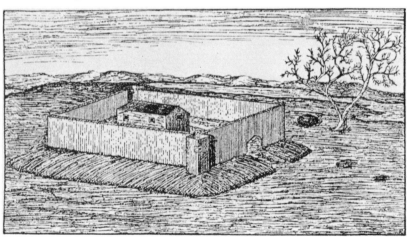

The land area of the Laconia Company was enormous. Listed on maps as the Province of Laconia, it officially included all land west of the New Hampshire grant, running to Lake Champlain, Lake Ontario and the St. Lawrence River. Neither Mason nor Gorges tried to develop this entire area. The grant was simply another part of the vast, ill-defined hinterland of the North American territory.

The Pannaway Plantation, by now abandoned, came under the Laconia Company's authority. According to Edward Hilton's Squamscot Patent, much of this same land belonged to the Dover Neck settlement as well. However, the land grants in New Hampshire were so complicated that they were actually ignored by those settlers who wished to put claim to the land. The territory was so vast, and settlements so few, that land ownership depended more on real people living in real houses than upon written grants from English sovereigns.

Captain John Mason, to whom New Hampshire now virtually belonged, never visited the colony. However, he did take a very deep interest in it. In 1631, he sent eighty emigrants in a ship called the *Pied Cowe,* to settle near the present site of Portsmouth. There they built the third, and what was to become the most important, settlement in the colony.

About three miles up the Piscataqua River from David Thomson's Pannaway, a man named Henry Chadbourne constructed "Great House," the first permanent structure to be erected in the area. On the banks of the river north and west of Great House grew tremendous patches of wild strawberries. Because the settlers had arrived during the spring season when the strawberries were in full fruit, they named their settlement "Strawbery Banke."

The community of Strawbery Banke quickly flourished. Although Great House had been built by Chadbourne, this building and the thousand acres of marshes, meadows, open fields and pastures surrounding it were still owned by the company—and the company supported the settlement well.

In 1632, a year after the settlement was chartered, Mason sent a herd of Danish yellow cattle to the colony, and by 1635, old records tell us, there were 24 milk cows, 34 head of other cattle, 92 sheep, 27 goats, 64 hogs and 21 horses on the plantation.

A list of provisions at Strawbery Banke in 1635 shows that the colonists were well equipped for life in the new country. They owned 89 guns, 61 swords, 13 barrels of gun-powder and about 1,000 pounds of bullets and shot, as well as the usual stores of corn, meal, oatmeal, malt, sugar, to-bacco, wine and brandy. The furnishings of Great House included flutes and two drums; some 1,276 pewter utensils such as bowls, plates, mugs, spoons and pitchers; and 15 pounds of candles to supplement the light of roaring fires and pine knots that guttered and flickered as they burned.

Work went quickly in the colony, and by 1635, two more houses had been built, and sawmills and saltworks had been established. In only four years, Strawbery Banke had grown from a wild field into a bustling community that was well on its way to becoming a self-sufficient town and a model for future settlements throughout New Hampshire.

In 1653, twenty-two years after the settlement had begun, the inhabitants decided that Strawbery Banke was too simple a name for their growing town. They petitioned the Massachusetts General Court for definite township, and the privilege of taking a new name, the name of Portsmouth. In part, the petition stated:

. . . may please this hon'd Court to take our case into consideration; and to consider of our extreme necessity, first in respect to the number of families, which are be-tween fifty and sixty, of w'ch some are constrained to remove from one of land to accomodate them with their stocks . . . we humbly intreat honor'd Court to take into theire view this necke of land w'ch we live upon; w'ch nature itselfe hath bounded with the maine, sea and river, as may be seen by the draft of the river, w'ch was presented to the last gen'l Court . . . the desire of yr humble petit'rs is, at this hon'd Court would grant us the necke of land. . . . And, whereas the name of this plantation att present being Strabery Banke, accidently soe called, by reason of a banke where strawberries *was* found in this place, now we humbly desire to have it called Portsmouth.

The town was ready for this physical expansion and more dignified name. The population had grown, and industry had been established. In 1640 an Anglican parish had been founded, with the Reverend Richard Gibson coming in as first pastor. Portsmouth won its township and continued to expand. The first meetinghouse was built in 1658. It was sixty feet long and thirty feet wide, and its two-and-one-half stories and high, pitched roof must have given the settlement an imposing skyline.

By the late 1650s, Portsmouth was already by far the most important and well developed town in the colony, despite the fact that the settlements at Pannaway and Dover had been established earlier.

It is interesting to note that in and near Portsmouth today there are still many families descended from the first fifty-eight men and twenty-two women who came over from England on the *Pied Cowe*. People named Camock, Gibbons, Joslin, Lane, Neal, Norton, Raymond, Vaughn, Waterton or Williams may be descendants of Captain John Mason's stewards. Fernalds may be descended from Renald Fernald, who was Mason's surgeon. People named Cooper, Chadbourne, Mathews, Knight, Langstaf, Walford, Moore, Herd or Rand may have ancestors who came to the colony as workmen or servants.

Back in 1635, when four-year-old Strawbery Banke was

thriving and twelve-year-old Dover Neck was sadly sending away the minister it couldn't support, a new settlement was being planned not far from Dover, at Squamscot Falls. It was to be called Exeter. Unlike the earlier settlements, which had been the result of grants from either the Council for New England or the king, Exeter was established on land purchased in 1635 directly from the Indians who then lived there.

The founder of the Exeter settlement was John Wheelwright. Wheelwright had been a preacher at Braintree, Massachusetts, and he was a brother of the controversial religious leader, Anne Hutchinson. In his agreement with the Indians, Wheelwright promised to make a settlement at Squamscot Falls within ten years. In 1638, he and a number of his followers began a "plantation" there.

Wheelwright and his people formed themselves into a church. They judged themselves completely separate from the legal authority of the Massachusetts Bay colony, which then governed all the New Hampshire settlements, and they formed their own political body and chose their own governors. The people of Exeter were solemnly sworn to obey these officers, who in turn were sworn to the due discharge of their duty. Laws were made by an assembly of the townspeople and were formally recognized by the governing body. The first governors were Isaac Grosse, Nicholas Needham and Thomas Wilson, each remaining in office for one year.

The Exeter settlement was well run and orderly, and its location at Squamscot Falls was an excellent one. However, it had no wealthy sponsors from outside its own boundaries, and Exeter grew slowly. By 1680 there were only a hundred families in the town.

About the same time that Wheelwright began negotiations with the Indians at Squamscot Falls, an outpost was established at Winnicunet, later called Hampton. Residents of neighboring Massachusetts had seen the salt marshes in

*John Wheelright,
founder of the Exeter
settlement*

the area, and they decided that Winnicunet was quite a valuable piece of land. In 1638, Richard Dummer and John Spencer were sent there to build a house at public expense. The cost was to be refunded once settlement was made. A building called the Bound House was erected, saltworks were established and herds of cattle were brought to the settlement to feed upon the salt hay.

That same year, a number of people from Norfolk, England, petitioned the General Court for the formal right to settle at Winnicunet. The permission was granted, and they, too, set to work on the settlement in a very efficient and well-organized manner. They began by laying out a township of 147 lots and forming a church under the ministry of the Reverend Stephen Bachiler, who became a prominent religious and civic figure in the New England colonies.

By the end of the first year, fifty-six people were settled in Winnicunet. The following year, they petitioned the

General Court to change the name of the town to Hampton. Permission was granted, and Hampton grew slowly but steadily throughout the seventeenth century. It was chiefly known for its saltworks and great fishing banks.

The precise way in which each of these four towns was settled, as well as the reasons for which a particular site was chosen for development, naturally varied from community to community. Yet, in many ways, the four towns were quite similar to each other in the general pattern of their development. In each town, for instance, the settlers soon established well-thought-out, specific rules for their own government. Also, each community had a church with a locally supported minister as part of its official government contract.

Uniting the towns even more closely was the fact that nearly all of the settlers had come from either neighboring parts of England or from nearby settlements in Massachusetts. This common bond proved to be particularly important during a later period when New Hampshire temporarily became a part of Massachusetts. It was a strong factor in the growth and development of the colony, and in the ultimate creation of New Hampshire as a separate colonial entity.

Home Life in Colonial New Hampshire

To the first settlers arriving in the New Hampshire colony, the coastline of the Great Bay, with its wide salt marshes, tidal creeks and deep forests, must have seemed a difficult place to try to set up a new home.

The raw materials were all there—heavy blue clay to be used as mortar; granite boulders to be laid in foundations or walls; plenty of timber to be hewn into beams, cut into boards or split into shingles, for floors, walls or roofs. At first the settlers were not sure exactly how these raw materials should be used or what sort of shelter would provide the best protection from both the weather and the possible danger of Indians or wild animals.

The first colonists in Pennsylvania had managed to live in caves cut into the banks of the Schuylkill River. The early Plymouth colonists had lived in flimsy mud and straw huts that caught fire or that melted when the rain was heavy. The New Hampshire settlers at Pannaway and later at Strawbery Banke were more fortunate, though. They were able to build substantial, fairly comfortable houses that provided satisfactory shelter for a number of years.

Since no pictures of these early homes survive, we can only guess at their appearance. We do know, however, that an enormous fireplace, large enough for a man to stand in or for a whole ox to be roasted in, was the center of each home. The home life and much of the handicrafts of the colony revolved around these hearths for many generations.

No stores or even trading posts existed in the early settlements, and if the colonists wanted anything that could not be made by hand, they had to wait for it until the ships arrived for the fishing season or until a boatload of new settlers came from home. Such common household goods as nails, tools, glassware and china were treasured as luxuries. The early colonists often used wooden pegs instead of nails and made wooden plates, bowls and spoons. They split the horns of cattle to make drinking glasses and kitchen utensils. They learned to make sugar from the sap of the maple tree, and they lighted their homes with pine splints, bear grease or bayberry candles. In general, they depended on either the raw materials from the natural resources of the countryside or on their own livestock and crops.

The new settlers made good use of the wild game in the forests, as well as the fish that were so plentiful on the coast and in the streams. They quickly learned to cultivate the Indian maize, or corn, which was unknown in the England of their day. The friendly Indians who camped up and down the Great Bay creeks taught the first settlers how to plant and raise the corn, as well as how to prepare it. Hominy, pone, samp and succotash, all new dishes to Englishmen, quickly became the staples of the New Hampshire diet.

A reconstructed colonial kitchen

Most of these foods were made from corn that had been ground in a wooden mortar or a hollowed stone. These mortars were pounded with a heavy block of wood called a pestle, and they could be heard for a great distance. A story has been told about two New Hampshire pioneers whose clearings were a quarter of a mile apart, and separated by a deep ravine and thick woods. In order for the two families to visit each other, they had to travel a long and roundabout trail, so the wives developed a code by which they could signal and communicate with each other every day as they pounded on their mortars.

Hand mills for grinding grains soon partially replaced the mortar and pestle, and in the middle of the seventeenth century they were followed by windmills and water mills. Water mills were used throughout the colonial period and well into the nineteenth century to grind meal and flour.

Pumpkins were another important crop to the colonial farmer. Although his fields were often studded with the enormous stumps of recently felled trees, he was still able to grow pumpkins in such land. Once grown, they could be kept easily for long periods of time in the deep, dry cellars under colonial houses. Pumpkins were used in many ways. The rind could be dried, ground in a mortar or mill and mixed with Indian corn to make pumpkin bread. It could also be stewed, and for many weeks in the early spring they often were the only vegetable available to many families.

The potato was originally an American plant that had been introduced to England by the first Virginia explorers and came to be called the "Virginia potato." It was reintroduced in America by the Scotch-Irish immigrants who came to New Hampshire around 1718, and that is how we came to have "Irish" potatoes. According to one popular New Hampshire recipe, the potatoes were cooked with butter, sugar and grape juice, mixed with various spices and then covered with a frosting of sugar.

Beans were also a popular food, and no New England Saturday night supper was complete without a pot of beans that had baked overnight in the brick oven. In religious New Hampshire households, cold baked beans were often the only food eaten on the Sabbath, when cooking would have been a breach of religious custom.

Farming in New Hampshire was a difficult business at best. The fields were often scarred with granite outcroppings and stubborn stumps that could not be pulled out, even by strong teams of oxen, until they had been left to decay for several years. The farmer had to do the best he could, so he planted small patches of corn, potatoes and other crops in order to keep his family alive during the bitter winter months.

A few farmers were fortunate enough to obtain some acreage that had already been cleared by the Indians, or a small plot of land that had been swept clean by nature in a forest fire or a wind storm. Such lands, however, were hard to find.

During the early colonial period, most farmers were content with getting enough food out of their land to keep their own families from going hungry. Thrifty farmers who cleared their land systematically, fertilized regularly and got rid of stumps as soon as possible were able to plant large fields of root crops, as well as rye, corn and hay. These farmers were soon able to export parsnips, beets, corn and, later, potatoes.

Since the original settlers in New Hampshire had come from southern England, where cider was a favorite drink, they often planted apple and pear orchards. These trees grew well, and cider was soon as popular in New Hampshire households as it had been in England, with great quantities exported. Also produced was a drink called perry, which was similar to cider, but made from pears instead of apples. This drink was especially popular in the Piscataqua area.

Other fruits were not cultivated to a great extent, but cherries, mulberries, plums and quinces were occasionally grown, sometimes in large enough quantities to be sent to Portsmouth or other coastal towns for sale or barter.

The Danish yellow cattle that John Mason had sent to Portsmouth during the first year of the Strawbery Banke settlement multiplied so well that, with the introduction of horses, sheep and other strains of cattle, the raising of livestock eventually developed into a profitable venture. In an economy centered around the sea, animal products such as leather, dried beef and salt pork could readily be developed for profit.

In the fall, when farmers butchered their herds, great barrels were filled with smoked dried beef and salt pork, which were then sold to the ships at Portsmouth Harbor to be used either by the British navy or by private merchant sailors. Any leather not used for clothing or shoes at home was also sold, and the hide of a New Hampshire cow or horse might find itself on London feet less than a year after its departure from a New Hampshire farm.

One of the earliest crops planted by the New Hampshire colonists, as soon as stones and stumps were cleared from their fields, was flax for linen. But linen cloth could actually be produced only after a long and complicated process. Flax was planted in May, pulled out by the roots when harvested in June or July and laid carefully in the fields to dry for several days. It was then soaked in a brook or stream for four or five days, and after the rotting leaves had been removed it was dried again and tied into bundles.

Strong men broke the fibers on a flax-brake, separating the fibers and removing the center core. After the flax had been broken twice, it was ready for "swingling"—a process that removed any small particles of bark or dirt that might still remain after all that soaking and drying. When this was done, the flax was pulled through large iron combs, called hackles, to divide the fibers into fine threads.

These fine threads or filaments were then spun on a small wheel by the farmer's wife, wound into skeins and then laid in warm water for four or five days, during which time they were frequently wrung out. Then the skeins were washed until the water ran through them pure and clear. But the thread was not yet ready for weaving. First it had to be bleached with lye and hot water or with slaked lime and buttermilk. Then, finally, it could be woven into fine white linen cloth. This cloth was used for making household sheets, towels, tablecloths, shirts, underclothing and dresses.

The production of linen was a difficult craft, but even though so much work and skill went into it, the colonial housewife was not able to turn her talents at the spinning wheel into a trade. She had no time. When she wasn't preparing food for immediate use by her family, or preserving pumpkins, apples, beans and other kinds of food for the long winter, she was washing clothes, spinning flax and wool, weaving cloth and cutting and sewing clothes for every member of the family.

In every town, the Congregational meetinghouse was one of the most important buildings. During the early colonial period, the word church meant "the congregation of the people," and the meetinghouse was the building in which the church, or the people, met. Unlike many churches today, the meetinghouse did not remain idle from Sabbath to Sabbath. It was a place where all kinds of gatherings were held. Usually, it was the only building where the entire population of a village could be seated. Various courts were held there, and so was the town meeting. The first meetinghouses were large, square buildings. They usually did not

The Congregational meetinghouse was both a church and a place where most town business was conducted

have bell towers, and they looked more like large houses than like churches as we know them today. The oldest meetinghouse still standing in New Hampshire is the one at Newington, which has been used continuously since 1713.

The Education Act of 1647 required a school to be set up in every town. Most children attended, but not many went beyond grammar school. Some New Hampshire boys attended Harvard College in Massachusetts, and a few went to England to study for the ministry.

One of the most prominent educators in New Hampshire was the Reverend Eleazer Wheelock. Rev. Wheelock was widely known for his work in educating Indian boys in

Connecticut, and in 1770, New Hampshire Governor John Wentworth, who had long been interested in Indian education, offered Wheelock a large tract of land for the purpose of founding a school. The school that Wheelock founded was Dartmouth College, the first college in the New Hampshire colony.

The place selected for the college was in the town of Hanover, at a spot four hundred feet above the level of the nearby Connecticut River. It was covered with immense pine trees, and although a clearing of six acres was made, the trees in the surrounding forest were so tall that the sun's rays did not penetrate to the floor of the clearing until afternoon.

Construction was started in August, 1770, and at the end of September, when there was still nothing but a temporary log cabin ready for use, the president's family and about thirty students arrived. They had traveled through the forest, over almost impassable roads, up the swift running river, enduring many hardships. Now, at the end of their journey, they had to sleep outdoors for almost a month, although the winter season had already begun, and there were rainstorms and snowstorms as early as October first. To add to the difficulties, the two sawmills on which Wheelock depended for lumber suddenly failed. Finally, by December 1, after a series of other disappointments, the president's house and the first building were completed. From then on, things went so well that, only four years later, the college was able to build Dartmouth Hall, a sturdy white brick Georgian structure that still serves as the principal building for Dartmouth College.

The college program was much shorter in those days than it is today, and the first class of students was graduated in the spring of 1771. The graduation was an occasion of great celebration in the Connecticut River valley. Not only the college trustees but Governor John Wentworth himself, as well as a number of his councilmen, made the trip from Portsmouth for the occasion.

To make the journey pleasant, or even possible at that time of the year, Governor Wentworth had a road built from Portsmouth to Hanover. It was known as the Dartmouth College Road, and it covered a distance of over one hundred miles—mostly over a rocky wilderness that was dotted with swamps, fallen trees and other obstacles. The graduating class consisted of four students.

Despite the prestige of the institution, a Dartmouth education in those days was not much more advanced than a high school education of today. Professional men learned their trade not by going to school but by reading in the office of a lawyer or by working beside a doctor. It was only the fortunate few, usually those who planned to enter the ministry, that were able to attend college for the full term. Generally, anyone who had taken a term or two at a private academy or at Dartmouth was considered a well-educated man indeed in colonial New Hampshire.

It was quite a major undertaking to go away to school, or, for that matter, to go anywhere outside one's own village. The first road from Portsmouth to Boston was not completed until 1700, and, until then, those few who did travel outside one of the few towns did so mostly by water. Many families owned small sloops or other boats that could navigate both the Great Bay and the tidal creeks.

In winter, when the waterways were frozen, travel was much more difficult. Sleighs and sleds were the only vehicles that could be used on the icy rivers and snow-covered roads. In the spring, travel was impossible, for the roads themselves became great mires and swamps. The few coaches and wagons that existed were easily bogged down in mud to the hubs of their high wheels.

It was not until 1761 that the first regular stage route was opened between Boston and Portsmouth. After the French and Indian War, many more roads were built, starting at the seacoast towns and inching inland.

Even the roughest roads, though, were a boon to the distribution of mail. Post riders, following Indian trails, animal trails and cow paths went between the towns as early as 1691. Even before the first road to Boston in 1700, a post route had been organized all the way from Portsmouth to New Castle, Delaware. Actually, post riders traveled the length of this route infrequently, and they carried messages that were often many months old, sometimes to or from people who had been dead for some time.

Along these early paths, trails and roads, a number of taverns were established. Often, these were little more than farmhouses whose owners would spread straw or cornhusk pallets on the floor in front of the kitchen hearth or move their children from a bed to accommodate those rare travelers who might have need of shelter. Taverns also served as

Dartmouth College was the first college in the New Hampshire colony

local meeting places, and much news was exchanged by local farmers and tradesmen who might gather in the common room for cider or ale after a busy day.

Life in New Hampshire was essentially rural. Trading and fishing were carried on in the coastal towns, but most of the colonists lived either in isolated groups or on even more isolated wilderness farms. As the colony grew, great industry flourished, especially in cutting trees and fishing. There were no shops or factories to produce manufactured goods, though, and throughout the colonial period, the New Hampshire colony was totally dependent on England and the continent of Europe for luxuries, and a "luxury" was almost anything that was manufactured.

Families existed by the efforts of their own hands. Most men were self-supporting, dependent upon their hands and their land to provide what was needed to feed, clothe and house their families. No salary or paycheck was earned by working for others. A living had to be made from a farm, or in the woods or on the sea. Goods were traded for goods and cash was seldom seen.

With the coming of better transportation in the early eighteenth century, the people of New Hampshire came to know more about their neighbors. Throughout the colonial period, however, New Hampshire was a fairly isolated place. The fact that it was dependent on no other colony fostered an independent spirit for which its men have been famous ever since.

Some of these men were industrious and thrifty, and were quickly successful. Others found little satisfaction in tilling a rocky hillside farm or owning a small fishing boat. These men moved constantly on and made their contribution by opening up the entire state for settlement by the late eighteenth century. Later, as these men moved north and west, they established a pattern of American development that was to continue until the mid-nineteenth century.

5

Fish, Furs and Trees

From its very beginning, the economy of the New Hampshire colony was based on three major industries: fishing, furs and the ship mast trade.

The early settlers came to New Hampshire for a variety of reasons. Some were excited by the possibility of owning land. Others hoped to set up a small business or trade or even to acquire a fortune in commerce. On the whole, though, it was fishing, more than anything else, that enticed the greatest number of Englishmen and Continentals to New Hampshire.

Even as far back as the beginning of the sixteenth century, sailors from the European continent had discovered the great banks of codfish and pollock off the New England coast. They already knew about the rich catches to be found in the deep waters of Great Bay and surrounding the Isles of Shoals.

As early as the summer of 1615, there were four hundred

French, Italian and Portuguese ships frequenting the North Atlantic shallows and two hundred English ships were reported in the area at the same time. Fishing was an extremely profitable venture, and there was a lot of competition. The first ship to arrive at a new area or to drop anchor in a harbor had the right to choose where the other ships from its country might fish, and frequently barred latecomers from the best spots.

The first thing the Thomson colonists did at Pannaway was to build a number of fish flakes, or drying racks, in preparation for the rich runs of cod and pollock that they expected to catch in the deep waters just outside Little Harbor. Later settlements, on the Isles of Shoals, and at Newcastle, Portsmouth, Rye and Hampton, also had their fish flakes, set up either by private individuals or by small fishing companies. The dried salt cod was sold either to visiting traders or through some Portsmouth merchant. By 1671, the annual export of fish from New Hampshire waters amounted to ten thousand quintals, or one million pounds of fish per year! And the catch doubled or tripled within the next half century.

Strangely enough, the Indians who had inhabited the inlets and creeks of the Great Bay area had little interest in salt-water fishing. They knew about the large schools of fish in the deep waters, but they preferred fresh-water fish, such as the salmon that spawned up the rivers and the tasty trout of inland lakes and streams.

The ocean-fishing industry was completely European in origin, developed by those adventurous shipowners and captains who brought their small, frail vessels to the northern Atlantic waters in the early sixteenth century. Those fishermen were the true pioneers of early New England.

Later the fishermen of colonial New Hampshire carried on their work in small whaleboats or slightly larger schooners. During the winter, the boats went out each morning and returned the same night. In the warmer months, the men stayed out longer, returning only when their boats were filled. The schooners generally made only three long trips per season. So the fish caught on a schooner had to be split and salted on board, and then stored in the hold. When the boat was finally unloaded, the fish were rinsed in salt water and then spread on the flakes. In clear weather, the fish were dried on top of the flakes, which were made of small saplings and twigs, raised from three to four feet above the ground. In bad weather, the catch was laid underneath the flakes. In either case, the fish were never allowed to be wet again until boiled for the table.

Only the boneless meat of the fish was dried on the flakes, but many other parts of the fish were also put to profitable use. Cod-liver oil was preserved in casks and boiled down for use in the tanning of leather. Fish tongues were pickled, and the heads of those fish caught in the smaller boats and brought directly home were used either as food for hogs or as fertilizer.

By the time of the American Revolution, seven or eight ships a year were leaving Portsmouth with cargoes of dried fish for Spain and Portugal. Most ships operating in and out of the harbor, however, were generally not used for transatlantic trade. Most often they were loaded with lumber, fish, oil, various types of livestock and rum made at Exeter, Dover or nearby Newmarket and then sent to the British Islands in the Caribbean. Two or three times a year, a ship was also sent to the French or Dutch West Indies.

When a ship arrived at its destination, the cargo was sold and the ship's hold was refilled with sugar and other products of the southern climate. Usually these goods were brought directly back to Portsmouth. Occasionally, though, a ship would go on to England from the Caribbean, then return to New Hampshire from the mother country loaded with glass, china, furniture, books and other manufactured products that were difficult or impossible to make in New Hampshire.

One vessel a year might go to the Azores, a group of islands west of Portugal, loaded with a cargo of wooden barrel staves, fish and other produce. Payment for this shipment would often be made partially in cash and partially in a return cargo of wines. On other occasions, a ship might go directly to England with lumber products and return with manufactured goods.

Despite the great variety in early New Hampshire trade, all of it can be traced directly back to the quantity and quality of the fish in the New Hampshire waters and to the industrious individuals who quickly turned these fish into an export product.

Before the American Revolution, the fishing trade was a great source of income both to the colonists and to their associates in England. During the Revolution, though, the trade broke down, and it was never fully revived.

The New Hampshire Indians, by nature a peaceful, friendly and curious people, quickly noticed the many interesting and useful objects that were brought to the New Hampshire coast by fishermen, traders and settlers.

For generations, the Indians had been attracted to the coat of the beaver, and the beaver skin was already an accepted medium of exchange among them by the time the first white men reached the New Hampshire shores. Fascinated by bright blankets, guns and the many other colorful objects that sailors had with them, the Indians offered to exchange beaver skins for European goods.

While the early beaver trade undoubtedly amounted to no more than casual deals with passing fishermen, it was not long before ships came especially to trade with the Indians for beaver furs. Other furs might have been as beautiful, and were probably easier to get, but the beaver skin was so much in demand in Europe that early traders in search of beaver opened many areas of New Hampshire that might otherwise have been unexplored until much later.

Almost every navigable creek in the Great Bay area was explored by fur traders early in the sixteenth century. Traders and, eventually, trappers penetrated deep into the New Hampshire forests, perhaps as early as the time of the first settlements at Dover and Portsmouth.

Traders rarely spent the winter on the coast, but arrived earlier than the fishermen, well fitted out with an assortment of knives, blankets, beads and guns, as well as large quantities of rum, for barter. John Smith tells of his luck in getting over five thousand beaver skins in a few weeks in 1614, even though his primary reason for visiting the coast was exploration, and it is unlikely that he was carrying any great quantity of goods for trade. By the second half of the seventeenth century, fur trade among both the French and the English became a major industry. We can only imagine the amazing numbers of beavers that gave up their lives so that some Indian might have a bright blanket or a string of glass beads, and some European gentleman might have a fine beaver hat.

Beavers were not the most important source of wealth that lay concealed in the depths of the New Hampshire forests. The forests themselves were vital to the economic development of the colony from the very beginning. The first settlers arriving at Pannaway, Dover, Exeter and other seacoast points were impressed by the great virgin woods that extended miles inland, covering the hills and mountains of the entire area. In these enormous forests, white pine trees often towered more than a hundred feet high before branches appeared, and their trunks might be as much as three or four feet thick.

To the seagoing British, these trees were an answer to a multitude of shipbuilding problems. The mainmast of an English naval ship of this period was a timber forty inches thick and forty yards long. From the early fifteenth century until the New Hampshire forests were opened, ship masts in England had been made by binding together several sections of Norwegian fir with iron hoops.

As early as 1634, New Hampshire white pines were taken to England to be made into masts. The trade did not start to flourish though, until about twenty years later, when the Dutch and the Danes cut off the supply of fir from Scandinavia. After that, however, the New England forests became a source of timber for the British navy for the next one hundred and twenty years, furnishing masts for all the largest vessels.

Early town records show that sawmills were among the first businesses set up in New Hampshire, and many family fortunes started with development of private wood lots and lumber yards. The mast trade quickly became a full-scale business venture in New Hampshire. It also created a need for a new and specialized kind of lumbering.

It took men of great skill and experience to cut down these enormous trees so that they would not break in their long fall. Several smaller trees were felled where their flexible branches would form a mat to break the fall of the large tree. This large tree might weigh from fifteen to twenty tons, and transporting it presented many problems.

Special "mast roads" had to be built over rocky hills and through swamps to carry the logs to some body of water large enough to float them to the Great Bay. These mast roads were the first straight highways to the sea, and many of them are still in use. Mast logs were taken out of the woods resting across the single axle of a pair of huge wheels that were high enough to raise a log above rocks and stones and swamp mud. As many as twenty yokes of oxen might be used to haul the loaded wheels to the waterside. In the winter, masts were drawn out of the forests on short, high sleds, two at each end of the log.

Once the log arrived at the river, it was "twitched" into the water and floated to mast pools from which it could be loaded onto ships. The ships came from England with a cargo of manufactured goods, and sailed from Portsmouth in the early spring, filled to capacity with these great trees. These "mast" ships had to be specially built so that the trees could be loaded through great doors or ports in the stern. The ships usually weighed from five hundred to one thousand tons, carried from forty to one hundred masts and were difficult to sail. Their arrival in Portsmouth Harbor, bringing mail, passengers, fine manufactured goods and other supplies from Britain were events noted often in the diaries of the colonists.

Early in the trade, a lively rivalry developed between the East India Company and the British navy for rights to the mast trees. Some New Hampshire fortunes, among them that of the famous Mark Hunking Wentworth, were developed through the bidding of the royal commissioners against the bids of the East India men. As the demand for the trees rose, great waste occurred. Mast trees were removed without concern for damage to nearby smaller trees. The developing trade in barrels, casks, barrel staves and other smaller timber products made it necessary to protect the mast trees against use for other purposes.

In 1685, restrictions were passed to prevent wasteful cutting. A surveyor general was appointed by the king, and under him worked privately employed surveyors who marked the mast trees with the King's Arrow—a mark

The King's Arrow was used to mark mast trees

shaped like a bird track and made with three blows of a hatchet. Almost all trees over twenty-four inches in diameter were under these restrictions by 1691. The restrictions created constant strife, and violations were common. Local officials often refused to cooperate with the king's representative and allowed mast trees to be cut into boards. To cover up the illegal act, such boards were never sawed more than twenty-three inches wide, which explains why many houses had floor and roof boards of twenty-two to twenty-three inches, but never the twenty-four-inch width that marked a tree for the King's use.

In addition to being the export center for the raw mate-

Ships were built in many New Hampshire towns along the seacoast and up the Piscataqua River

rials of the British mast trade, New Hampshire soon became a center of shipbuilding itself. Throughout the colonial period, New Hampshire produced over 17 per cent of the total tonnage of ships constructed in the colonies.

Ships were built in many New Hampshire towns along the seacoast and up the Piscataqua River and its tributaries. Sometimes shipyards were set on the banks of streams, but there are stories about ships of one hundred tons and more being built as far as one or two miles from the water. These ships were built in the warm months, drawn by strong teams of oxen over the frozen ground during the winter and then floated down the river in the spring. Men also told of ships having been built seven to eight miles from the seacoast, taken apart and carried by ox team to the sea.

New Hampshire craftsmen excelled in shipbuilding, and the ships they built were said to be some of the best to float in English waters. Shipping, the mast trade and the production of barrel staves were such big businesses in New Hampshire that by 1774, 14 million board feet of lumber were being taken from New Hampshire forests and exported through Portsmouth Harbor annually.

Forest products, furs and fish were by far the most important economic "crops" in New Hampshire during the colonial period.

6

Conflict with
Massachusetts and
England

When the boundaries of Massachusetts were officially established in 1629, the people who set them were operating under some false information. They believed that the Merrimack River, which begins near the shores of northern Massachusetts, flowed straight west, parallel to the present New Hampshire-Massachusetts border. The part of the river that was then known to explorers and settlers did just that. However, the rest of the Merrimack River does nothing of the kind. It makes a great curve northward and runs right up the center of New Hampshire. So, when Massachusetts was officially defined as all that land "within the space of three English miles to the northward of said river . . . or to the northward of any and every part thereof," all of what was then New Hampshire was automatically included in the Massachusetts charter.

This meant that the settlements existing in New Hampshire at that time came under the immediate jurisdiction of the Massachusetts Bay colony, and other settlements, established later in the same general area, were automatically a part of Massachusetts as well. In practice, this meant mainly that the Massachusetts General Court handled all of New Hampshire's important legal affairs. On paper, it meant that Massachusetts had the legal right to tell New Hampshire what to do. There were some influential people in Massachusetts who indeed wanted to exercise that right, even though New Hampshire settlers neither needed nor wanted Massachusetts control.

Massachusetts Bay was a rich and powerful colony, and it had a great number of settlers. To some of them, the idea of owning or living on land in wilder, more challenging New Hampshire was appealing. Others were simply greedy to claim New Hampshire's natural riches. So, in 1631, John Winthrop, the governor of the Massachusetts Bay colony, decided to make his paper claim to New Hampshire a fact.

Winthrop sent Captain Thomas Wiggin to take control of Dover. However, Wiggin received a rather icy welcome. He was met by Captain Walter Neale, who dared Wiggin to set foot on a certain point of land midway between Exeter and Dover. Wiggin, armed with his commission from the Massachusetts Bay governor, drew his sword and dared Neale to defend the settlers' rights by a duel. As it turned out, the quarrel ended without bloodshed, but the point of land that was defended by Neale is known to this day as Bloody Point.

Since force was obviously not the way to obtain possession of the Great Bay settlements, Wiggin tried a different approach. In 1632, he bought Edward Hilton's entire grant of land in Dover for a large sum of money. Now that he literally owned Dover, it was much easier for him to try to place the property of the settlers already living there under Massachusetts control. Needless to say, however, there were many citizens in Dover who objected to this idea just as strongly as they had before.

One of the strongest protesters of all was George Burnett, an English minister hired by Dover in 1636. From the time of his arrival, Burnett began stirring up the feelings of the townspeople against Wiggin, probably even to the point of spreading a number of rumors that weren't even true. Burnett was soon elected governor of the town, but he succeeded only in arousing the people further, and the situation did not improve. In fact, chaos continued in Dover for the next four years.

Finally, in 1640, the inhabitants of Dover, who had had no real government at all during this time, put aside their personal opposition to Wiggin and the Massachusetts Bay colony. They signed a document known as the Dover Combination, in which they agreed to submit to the laws of England, as well as any other laws that might receive a majority vote among them. The following year, all of the New Hampshire settlements were more or less willingly annexed to Massachusetts.

New Hampshire people were basically independent, though, and they were driven by a pioneering spirit that made it difficult for them to tolerate this union. Although troubled areas like Dover quieted down at first, the entire period of Massachusetts rule, from its beginning in 1641 to its end in 1679, was a time of great conflict.

One important cause of this conflict was disagreement about religious tolerance. Many settlers in the Great Bay towns were Anglicans, and there was constant bickering between them and the Massachusetts Puritans. Unlike the neighboring colonies of Plymouth and Massachusetts Bay, the early New Hampshire settlements were not founded primarily for religious reasons. In fact, the first church in New Hampshire was not organized until ten years after the Pannaway settlement had been established at Odiorne's Point.

This church was a Congregational church, founded in

Dover in 1633. By 1640, settlers at Strawbery Banke had established an Anglican parish, and it is unlikely that the Congregationalists minded this very much. Some religious tolerance existed very early in New Hampshire towns, but this was not so in Massachusetts. The Massachusetts Bay colony had been founded on the basis of strict Puritan doctrine, which did not allow for the toleration of other religious ideas or beliefs. When the New Hampshire towns, full of Anglicans and Congregationalists, came under the authority of the Massachusetts General Court, there was a great deal of discord over religion.

This conflict began on a large scale. As soon as the annexation was official, a great wave of Puritan settlers came into the New Hampshire region. Through the aid of Massachusetts officials, who had promised much religious and civic freedom to their own original settlers, these later Puritans received great tracts of unoccupied New Hampshire land. These grants resulted in open rebellion on the part of New Hampshire people, and towns attempted twice, in 1651 and in 1654, to withdraw from their union with the Massachusetts Bay Colony. Both attempts were unsuccessful.

Despite this conflict, some good did come to New Hampshire from her union with the Massachusetts Bay colony. Perhaps the most notable good was the exploration of certain parts of the Merrimack River valley. This exploration eventually led to the founding of Dunstable, the fifth major town in the colony, and the first New Hampshire town to be established in the interior, far from Great Bay.

In 1652, the Massachusetts General Court appointed commissioners to determine the northernmost point of the Merrimack River. Two surveyors, Simon Willard and Edward Johnson, worked their way up the river for four months, and finally, guided by local Indians, they arrived at the outlet of Lake Winnipesaukee. There, on a large boulder in the channel leading from the lake at the Weirs, the two men chiseled the name of Governor John Endicott, and the initials of his two commissioners.

Under the auspices of the Massachusetts Bay colony, exploration and the planning of settlements in the area moved quickly. In 1656, land on both sides of the Merrimack was surveyed, and many grants were made. One thousand acres were given to the town of Charlestown, Massachusetts, and other grants were awarded to various individuals, including Governor John Endicott.

In the spring of 1660, a few newcomers began arriving at the site of Dunstable. By 1662, several more grants had been made, including one to the "Ancient and Honorable Artillery Company" of Boston. By 1673, fourteen thousand acres along both sides of the Merrimack had been granted, but few settlements had actually been made by that time.

In September, 1673, proprietors of these lands, and others who wished to settle the area, petitioned the Massachusetts General Court to grant them a township. The township was granted on the conditions that twenty or more settlers would develop the area, that they would erect a meetinghouse and a fort by 1676 and that they would actually live upon and improve their land. Thus Dunstable became an official town. The name Dunstable came from "dun," a hilly place, and "staple," a market or store.

The township was huge, probably more than two hundred square miles. It included the present-day New Hampshire towns of Nashua, Hudson, Hollis and Dunstable, as well as a large portion of what is now Middlesex County, Massachusetts. The grant had been so large that, even though little land was settled, the eastern border of the township had to be extended.

By 1674, farms were already under cultivation, and the following year, apple orchards began to bloom. By 1676, the deadline set by the General Court, much had been accomplished. Trading centers had been set up for commerce with the Indians. Not only houses, but a schoolhouse and a garrison had been built, and streets laid out. Cornfields, orchards and gardens had been planted and fenced in, and cattle had been brought to the settlement. Dunstable was well on its way to becoming a prosperous, well-governed trading and agricultural community.

Soon after Dunstable had been fully established as the first major inland community in the New Hampshire territory, the union between New Hampshire and Massachusetts was dissolved. In 1679, New Hampshire was made into a royal province. It now came under the authority of the English king.

With its new status, New Hampshire underwent many changes. King James II appointed John Cutt, a resident of Portsmouth, president of the colony and established a council composed of prominent New Hampshire men. All but one of these men were representatives of the various settlements throughout the area. The one man who was not a representative was Robert Mason, heir to John Mason's claim to the New Hampshire territory, and he was a troublemaker.

Robert Mason managed to get onto the council simply because, during the annexation, he had made such loud and vigorous attempts to enforce his land claims that he could not be ignored. Once appointed to the council, Mason quickly won the favor of the king. With a royal warrant in hand, he came to New Hampshire to try to force the settlers to buy leases from him for the land they were already living on.

Mason was opposed by President Cutt and the entire assembly, and he had no success at all. He had still another scheme, however. He returned to England and made great promises of land, prestige and power for both king and council. All this would be obtained under the Masonian grants—if one Edward Cranfield were to be appointed royal governor of the province. Cranfield, who scarcely trusted Mason, even though he was well acquainted with him, accepted the appointment only after he had squeezed from Mason a personal guarantee that his salary would be paid and that he would be received in New Hampshire as befitted a royal governor.

When Cranfield arrived in New Hampshire, though, in 1682, he didn't receive the welcome he had asked for. His first actions as governor threw the colony into chaos at once. Using a list of names given him by Mason, Cranfield removed those men in high office who were opposed to the Masonian claims and appointed others of his choice. Even then, he failed to keep the colony under control. The people were violently opposed to Cranfield's attempts to make them honor the Masonian claims, and they refused to obey court decrees. They even refused to pay their taxes. Complaints of tyranny and nonrepresentation were sent to England, and in 1685, after three turbulent years, Cranfield was finally removed.

The colony probably rejoiced when the hated Cranfield was overthrown, but his replacement, Lieutenant Governor Barefoote, was just as bad. Barefoote had been appointed by Cranfield himself and used every means in his power to irritate and annoy the settlers. As for the colonists, they had little respect for royal government at this time. In fact, their respect was so low that two former assemblymen—that is, representatives of towns—Thomas Wiggin and Anthony Nutter, dared to call upon Barefoote at his home to complain about his injustices. They found in Barefoote's living room none other than Robert Mason, who happened to be the governor's house guest at the time.

Nutter and Wiggin fully informed Mason in plain language that his claim to New Hampshire amounted to little. Mason tried to force the two men to leave the house, but Wiggin, who was a very large man, grabbed Mason by the

*Thomas Wiggin and Anthony Nutter informed Lieutenant
Governor Barefoote that his claim to New Hampshire amounted
to little*

collar and threw him into the fireplace. Mason's clothing
and body were severely burned. Barefoote, who tried to help
Mason, fared just as badly. He lost several teeth and suffered
two broken ribs. Incidents such as these did little to improve
relations between Barefoote and the colonists. Barefoote
was soon relieved of his post, only to be followed by Joseph
Dudley, who a few months later was in turn sent back to
England.

In 1686, the Dominion of New England was created, and
James Andros was made governor of all the New England
colonies. Compared to Andros, his predecessors were merely
petty tyrants. Andros spent his entire term of office trying
to force the settlers to pay ridiculously high taxes. When
King James lost the throne in 1689, however, Andros was
captured and sent to England as a prisoner of the state.

Although the 1680s were a time of great discord between
the colonists and the royal government, the New Hampshire
assembly made many constructive moves toward the development of a self-governing colony. Perhaps their most

important action was the organization of a militia in the early 1680s. For the first time, the New Hampshire settlers had a sound military base for their protection from both royal governor and Indian alike. The assembly also set up voting procedures and compiled a set of laws that became the basis for the New Hampshire legal code throughout the colonial period.

After the removal of Andros, however, New Hampshire had no formal government at all, and the last ten years of the seventeenth century were troubled ones. The French in Quebec were constantly gaining more territory in the north and were stirring up the Abenaki Indians and other northern tribes, with the hope that they could scare the English colonists out of New England. The French wanted to claim the St. Lawrence Basin and the fertile river valleys of Massachusetts and New Hampshire for themselves.

Realizing the importance of rebuilding the militia, as well as living under a more stable form of government, the settlers of Dover, Exeter, Hampton and Portsmouth joined together. They sent delegates to a convention for the purpose of drawing up a constitution for the colony of New Hampshire. The Hampton delegation, however, disagreed with the others on several important matters. Hampton refused to comply with the proposed constitution, so the pact was useless.

It seemed that a break in the New Hampshire assembly might soon add to the troubles of the colony. There was a party that had always felt a bond with Massachusetts and wished to be reannexed to the Massachusetts Bay colony. This party now petitioned Massachusetts for aid and protection against the French and the Indians, who seemed more hostile every day. The petition was granted, and for a short time New Hampshire was once more reunited with Massachusetts.

The new union remained in effect until 1692, when

Lieutenant Governor John Wentworth worked hard for the general welfare of the province and its people

Samuel Allen obtained a royal commission and became governor of New Hampshire. Allen, however, spent little time in the colony, and almost everything that was accomplished during his term in office was done by his lieutenant governors. Through the beginning of the eighteenth century, most of the governors who followed Allen likewise gave most of their responsibilities to their lieutenants. Perhaps the most important of these lieutenant governors was John Wentworth.

Wentworth, a resident of Portsmouth, became the founder of a long line of important New Hampshiremen and public servants. During his term, he worked hard for the general welfare of the province and its people, and he was very well liked. His name and deeds formed the solid basis upon which his son, Benning, built the governorship of the New Hampshire colony into the important place it held in New England during the mid-eighteenth century.

7

The Settlements Expand

During the seventeenth century, the over-all development of New Hampshire was slow. Even though five major towns had been quite solidly established, there was actually very little other settlement in the colony, except for the few isolated farms and trappers' huts that dotted the wilderness.

Furthermore, nothing was really being done by the proprietors of land to encourage families to settle in the vast forested acres of valleys, hills and mountains that the early explorers had described with such awe and admiration. Roads were difficult to build on this kind of land, and farms were hard to establish. The few colonists who did choose to settle in New Hampshire made their homes along the tidal creeks and rivers that emptied into the Great Bay.

In the beginning of the eighteenth century, though, new waves of settlers began to push their way into New Hampshire, coming from England, Scotland and northern Ireland. These were the people who eventually formed the backbone of the New Hampshire colony and, later, the New Hampshire state.

Perhaps the most important group of immigrants to

arrive during this period were the Scotch-Irish, frugal Presbyterians who came from northern Ireland to settle in Londonderry, below Amoskeag Falls. They were successful tradesmen, thrifty farmers and skilled weavers who quickly made "Londonderry linen" a byword for fine workmanship. The Londonderry Scotch-Irish, in fact, attained such a high and widespread reputation that, in 1748, the selectmen of the town of Londonderry ordered that each bolt of cloth leaving the town be marked "Londonderry in New Hampshire." By 1768, the Londonderry linen weavers were producing over 25,000 yards of cloth a year.

When Benning Wentworth became governor in 1741, it was his goal to expand such industrial activities and to make New Hampshire one of the most important of the English colonies in North America. This was no easy task.

At the time he took office, the value of foreign trade amounted to only one-fifth that of the trade with other New England seaports. It was Wentworth's ambition to develop a thriving trade with England and the West Indies, in order to bring in the gold and silver that were so badly needed in New Hampshire. Such trade would make it unnecessary for the colony to print its own paper money. It would then also make it possible for shipbuilding to become an important industry along the shores of Great Bay. In fact, Wentworth hoped that once Portsmouth's shipbuilders were able to compete successfully with those of Newburyport and Salem, he might then secure contracts for the building of warships for the king's navy.

Benning Wentworth, however, did not set about to achieve his high goals for the benefit of New Hampshire and the king alone. He was ambitious for himself. He wanted his name to be known and to be associated with growth and westward expansion. He planned to develop New Hampshire as far west as he could, even if it meant pushing the colony's boundaries west of the Connecticut River.

Wentworth had kept his eye on the Scotch-Irish London-

Benning Wentworth became governor in 1741

derry settlements for a long time. In fact, he was so impressed by the hard work and success of these people that he decided to invite more emigrants from northern Ireland to come and settle in the western part of New Hampshire. In Pennsylvania, Wentworth knew, the Scotch-Irish and German immigrants had opened vast lands for farming and had contributed greatly to the growth and population of that colony. Wentworth hoped the same would happen in New Hampshire. Furthermore, the governor also knew that in the process of carving farms out of the wilderness, the settlers would also produce materials for use in shipbuilding, such as pitch, resin and mast wood for sale abroad.

Increasing the population of the colony, Wentworth realized, was extremely important. The more people who sought to settle on the land, the higher the land prices would go. Wentworth saw this as a great advantage to the king, whose benefit he held secondary to his own, but whose good graces were constantly on his mind.

Perhaps most important, though, Wentworth realized that if his new inland settlements were linked to Portsmouth (and incidentally to his far-reaching, influential family), untold wealth would be brought to New Hampshire. Wentworth had no intention of allowing the products of the rich farmlands and felled forests of the Merrimack and Connecticut river valleys to slip downstream on spring currents into the hands of rival colonists in Connecticut, New York and Massachusetts.

He insisted that the assembly grant funds for a road from Portsmouth to the Connecticut River, on which these products could be transported through the southern portion of the colony. This plan was never carried out to the extent that the governor hoped, but it indicated how urgently he felt that expansion of the inland towns should be encouraged.

During the first five years of his administration, Benning Wentworth took possession of a great deal of New Hampshire land. He took the lands that belonged to proprietors who had not been loyal to him, and he took land in towns where settlement had not taken place during a five-year period. As governor, Wentworth had the right to do this, but when the proprietary claims of the Masonian grant were sold, he was unable to do it any longer.

Robert Tufton Mason, the last descendant of John Mason, saw little possibility that his inherited claim to the rich New Hampshire hinterlands would be legally recognized, and in 1746 he sold the Masonian claims to twelve Portsmouth merchants for fifteen hundred pounds provincial money.

These new proprietors, ten of whom were related to the governor, and seven of whom were members of the governor's council, quickly divided the land among themselves. The assembly considered the bargain to be corrupt. Wentworth, on the other hand, saw nothing wrong with it. However, he was angry because the division had been made behind his back and, more important, because the new proprietors refused to sell him rights to the land. Wentworth brought suit against the landholders. Unfortunately for the governor, he was unable to get the land away from them legally.

Wentworth now had to look to the west for new lands to divide, grant and plant with the seeds of settlement. For two years, he watched enviously as great tracts of valuable land were divided up and sold for large profits. He was also frustrated by various rules from the Board of Trade. No land grants could be made until fifty families were willing to settle the area. No grants larger than fifty acres could be given to any individual. Wentworth felt that each grant should be between three hundred and five hundred acres and that, unless the limit were raised, neither he nor the king would live to see the colony developed to any extent.

Late in 1749, Wentworth began making grants of land in what is now Vermont. On November 17, he informed Governor Clinton of New York that he wished to grant "the unimproved lands within my government." Wentworth stated that the land now comprising Vermont, and not then claimed by New York, was New Hampshire territory. He decided that the dividing line between the two colonies would be a piece of land twenty-four miles from the Hudson River and six miles north of Massachusetts. He made this first grant and called it Bennington. New York protested, and Wentworth promised not to make any more grants on the western border of *his* colony so that he wouldn't interfere with the growth of New York.

Barely two weeks had passed before he did make another such grant, and the New Yorkers were quick to make official protest to the king and the council. Governor Clinton had not counted on the promptness of Wentworth's actions at a time when his own cause could be furthered, and he was informed by the Secretary of the Board of Trade that Wentworth had outmaneuvered him.

The uproar that followed these first two grants in the area west of the Connecticut made Wentworth a bit more cautious. He made only two grants in 1750, and two more in 1752. His cause was helped by King George's War in the early 1750s. Troops were constantly moving to and from the Connecticut River valley region, and many people became interested in this previously unexplored land. They saw it not only as rich farm land, but as a valuable area for speculation. Wentworth, too, realized how profitable the investment in this land could be, and he named a number of important Englishmen and colonists as proprietors of new towns to be laid out along the east and west banks of the Connecticut River.

Encouraged by his success and by the lack of complaint from the New Yorkers, he made seven grants in 1753, and three more in 1754. Wentworth was quick to tell everyone, both in writing and in conversation, that the only purpose in these grants was the good of the colony. He was not without his own interests, however. In each town, he reserved for himself a lot of five hundred acres as his fee for affixing the royal seal to the grant.

Each township covered an area of six square miles and was divided into seventy different shares. In addition to reserving his own land, Wentworth set aside shares for a school, the first settled minister, the Church of England and the Society for the Propagation of the Gospel in Foreign Parts. The grants to both the Propagation Society and the Anglican Church reflected Wentworth's eagerness to further the Anglican cause in New Hampshire. In actuality, though the governor was indirectly helping the cause of the Congregationalists more, since a New Hampshire town's first settled minister, whose share of land had been set aside by Wentworth, was almost always a Congregationalist.

Wentworth was more successful, though, in using his land grants to favor his large family. He looked out well for the claims of his relatives. In fact, most of the people who received grants from him were either related to him or were members of the assembly or council, even though some of them did not live in New Hampshire.

Even to his relatives, though, Wentworth did not make grants as simple gifts. Through the granting of land, he was able to bargain for support for other purposes. Before he left office in 1767, Wentworth had assigned 128 pieces of land west of the Connecticut River. In these 128 towns, Wentworth's relatives owned 365 tracts. Although no evidence exists, it is more than likely that these shares were not all given free. The extravagant tastes of the governor, and the enormous estate he left when he died in 1770, indicate that even members of Wentworth's family must have paid with more than loyalty for their privileges.

While Wentworth and his family profited greatly from these land grants, so did the colony of New Hampshire. One of Wentworth's major hopes was that influential proprietors would encourage colonists who had initially settled elsewhere to move to New Hampshire. In the long run, this idea worked. There were many people of all kinds who were eager to settle the newly established towns in what had recently been wilderness—but only after 1764, which was just three years before Wentworth retired.

Wentworth was not fortunate enough to see the flood of new settlers he had wished for, until the very end of his term as governor. There was one very big factor working against Wentworth's ambitions during almost the entire period of his governorship. That factor was Indian trouble. New Hampshire was very dangerous country up until the end of the French and Indian War in 1763, and people with the courage to move into such an area were few and far between.

8

Trouble with the Indians

Although the Indian attacks reached their peak in the French and Indian War, which started in 1754, they had been occurring throughout the colony from the very beginning of English settlement. The vast North American continent should have been large enough for the colonies of both England and France, but there was conflict over territorial ownership as early as the 1680s.

The French cleverly sought an ally in the Indians, some of whom had actually been harmed by the English, and were eager for revenge. The French also managed to persuade other Indians that the English were the enemy of the Indian race, while the French wanted only to protect the rights of the natives.

Small bands of Indians, encouraged by the French settlers of the northern New England coast, soon began to harass the English frontier settlements. In 1689, frontier raiding broke into open warfare. Governor Andros rashly stormed the fort of the leader of the French settlements, Baron de

St. Castine. Andros left only the silver ornaments in the chapel to console the Baron for the loss of the arms and goods of his colony.

Then the northern Indians suddenly swooped down into New Hampshire, complaining that their corn had been devoured by English cattle. Sachem Wonolancet, whose father, Sagamore Passaconaway, had ordered his people not to quarrel with the English, fled to Canada with some of his followers from the Pennacook and Pequawket Nation, and an angry warrior took his place.

Before long, the town of Dover was attacked. At the time, Dover consisted of several small water mills and five fortified houses surrounded by palisades. Basically, it was a trading center, and its people were used to seeing Indians passing through the town every day. Richard Waldron, the magistrate, was warned by some of the settlers and even by Indian squaws, that mischief was brewing, but he told his fellow townsmen to go and plant their pumpkins as usual. He promised he would let them know as soon as he expected Indian trouble to break out.

Unfortunately, by the time Waldron was convinced that there was trouble, he was in no position to warn anyone. On the evening of June 27, the five houses received visits from pairs of squaws, who asked if they might sleep by the fire. When everyone was asleep, the squaws stole to the doors, unbolted them and opened the gates to the palisades, allowing the Indians to enter. The Indians stunned Waldron with a hatchet, dragged him into his kitchen, tortured him horribly and then stabbed him to death with his own sword.

The other garrisons were overcome with the same kind of sudden brutality. Practically the entire settlement, including the mills, was burned, and the captives were quickly marched to the French settlements in Canada. This was the first attempt at using English prisoners for the purpose of ransom.

Other settlements in the New Hampshire territory were terrorized as well. After numerous raids, including an attack on Dunstable in September, 1691, the people of New England decided that French Canada was the source of their troubles. They were determined now to turn the Canadian colonies into English provinces, and they asked the mother country for help.

England sent Sir William Phipps to the colonies, and he began an unsuccessful expedition toward Quebec. But just when the situation seemed at its worst for the English, the Indians appeared with a flag of truce. The truce did not last long, however. In the next few years attacks continued with such force that, according to the council minutes, the people of New Hampshire once considered abandoning the province for good.

In March, 1694, the Indians struck again, this time at the settlement of Oyster River, which is now called Durham. There were twelve garrison houses at Oyster River. These houses were probably large enough to protect all of the families in the town, but on the evening before the attack the Indians approached undetected. They formed two divisions, one to go up each side of the river, and planted themselves in ambush near every house. The attack began early the next morning, when John Dean, a local resident, got up before daybreak to go on a long trip. As he opened his door to leave his house, Dean was immediately shot and killed.

Although the town was alarmed by the sound of the shot, the ambush parties were so well prepared that there was no time for defense. Five of the twelve garrisons were destroyed. The Indians set fire to nearly all the houses, and the people who survived were forced to flee for their lives.

These vicious attacks, including the Haverhill raid of 1697, in which Mrs. Hannah Dustin was captured, kept the colony in a constant state of fear. In an effort to protect themselves, the colonists built Fort William and Mary at the entrance to Portsmouth Harbor on the island of New Castle, in hope that at least the coastal section of the colony might not be devastated.

Queen Anne's War, between 1702 and 1713, brought more troubles to the already disillusioned and frightened colonists. A new series of attacks threw New Hampshire into a state of terror and confusion. Women and children were confined to forts, and men had to have military guards in order to work safely in the fields.

In 1712, though, New Hampshire launched its first successful counterattack, led by the famous scout Thomas Baker. Also, a year earlier, the New Hampshire assembly had encouraged the colonists to attack by placing a bounty on Indian scalps. According to the bounty law, the scalper would be rewarded as follows: "for every Male of Twenty years old and Upward, Sixty pounds, for Every Woman Indian, thirty pounds, for Every Minor, fifteen pounds."

If things were so bad in such well-established towns as Dover and Dunstable, one can imagine that life in the western outposts of the colony was even more difficult. In fact, from the beginning of the eighteenth century until the end of the French and Indian War in 1763, the western settlers had to work just as hard to protect themselves from the Indians as they did to set up their homes.

Between 1715 and 1725, intense fighting, known as Father Ralé's War, was concentrated in the area east of the Merrimack River, in the present state of Maine. During this time, the French and the Indians used the broad, smooth currents of the Connecticut River as a highway, which allowed them to swoop down quickly from the north and attack the isolated New Hampshire settlements on their way to Maine.

With the threat of such vicious and sudden attacks, it was little wonder that colonists hesitated to settle near the banks of the Connecticut River.

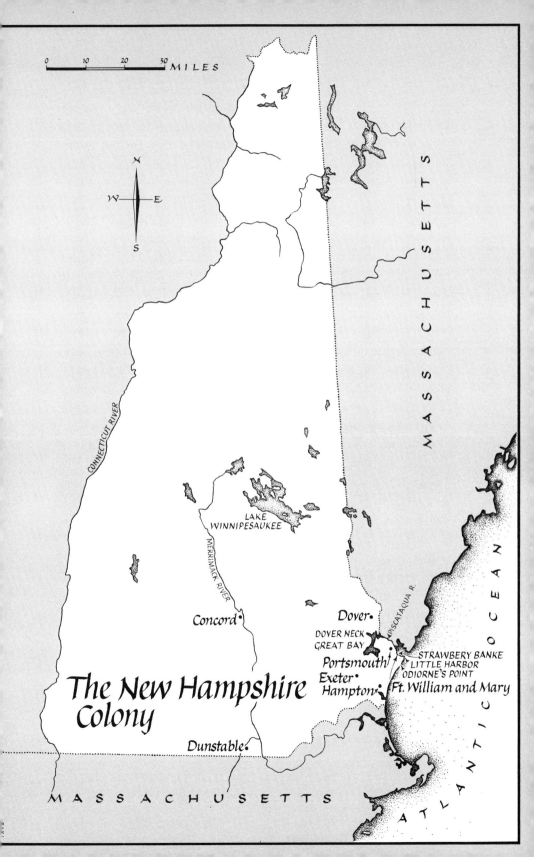

The New Hampshire Colony

On July 15, 1720, war was officially declared against the Indians. Soon afterward, the bounty on Indian scalps was increased to one hundred pounds for every Indian male, female or child. On August 17, 1724, New Hampshire sent out an expedition of two hundred men to move north against the Norridgewock Indians. The expedition was highly successful, and Father Ralé, the Frenchman responsible for stirring up so many Indians, was killed.

Yet, even after Father Ralé's War was over, the country remained uneasy. Any settler who thought about moving to the rich meadowlands of the Connecticut River valley, knew that there was still a good chance that his entire family might be killed there, or taken to Canada for ransom. But in spite of the dangers, new settlements were planned. Land was explored and surveyed, and in 1735, twenty-eight towns were plotted between the Merrimack and Connecticut rivers, and two more were planned on the west side of the Connecticut River.

The most famous of these Connecticut River towns to actually be settled around this time were four forts, called by their numbers. One through Four, instead of by names.

The men and women who settled these forts and towns, unlike the colonists who had braved the wilderness fifty or a hundred years earlier, were already Americans—people whose parents and grandparents had brought the first aspects of a permanent white civilization to western Massachusetts and Connecticut. In the true pioneer spirit, these people were ready to move on as soon as their farms were cleared. In 1740, three pioneering families from Lunenburg, Massachusetts, toiled up the river with their supplies and began the settlement of Fort Number Four. The next year, John Kilburn, originally of Weathersfield, Connecticut, left Northfield, Massachusetts, and started a "plantation" at Fort Number Three. Soon after that, the first settler arrived at Fort Number One.

For the first few years, these fort settlements were generally secure and quiet, but in 1744 the Indians struck so suddenly and viciously that most of the western New Hampshire settlements were abandoned. Their inhabitants left behind the log huts and small farms that they had carved out of the wilderness and returned to the safety of less-isolated communities. Only a fortified blockhouse at Fort Number Three and a remote settlement at Fort Number Four remained occupied in a long strip of abandoned farms along the broad Connecticut.

To call the weak settlement at Fort Number Four a fort is being generous. After seven years of occupation, it remained merely a thin stockade of logs, actually only a fence, connecting six houses. These houses formed a rough quadrangle, and in the center stood a crude watchtower. Twenty-four hours a day, there was a guard posted in the tower, prepared to warn the settlers of an approaching enemy. The six houses were small and unfinished, but at one end of the fort there was a great barracks hall for the troops of resident soldiers who did not have homes and families in the town. There were also two wells in the center of the fort.

The troops at Fort Number Four were neither well armed, well equipped, nor well trained. Most of the men were farmers who knew nothing of marching or military procedure. They knew no more about how to be soldiers than what they had learned from the scouting and woods fighting they had done to protect their own homes. The captain of the group was not a trained British regular, but an American farmer named Phineas Stevens.

The size of the fort itself was pitifully small. It included only twenty to thirty men and a few dogs. Against this tiny fort, the French sent an army of several hundred Indians and Frenchmen sweeping down the valley.

On April 7, 1747, the day was cold and clear. As the sun rose, the man standing guard outside the gate noticed that several of the mongrel dogs were moving uneasily in the frosty air. The dogs whined and growled, and made short runs back and forth to the woods. The guard, with his gun in hand, finally followed the dogs into the woods. He heard no sound, but felt certain that he was surrounded by Frenchmen and silent Indians. Suddenly, fire burst from the woods. The guard raced back to the fort, and the attack began. The attacking force consisted of well-trained French and Indian warriors—probably from four hundred to seven hundred of them—led by the French General Dabeline.

Sure that the fort was poorly manned, they now rose from ambush and began a furious attack from all sides. Captain Stevens and his thirty men stood firm at each post, loading and firing rapidly and beating the attackers back with sharp plays of musket fire. The siege lasted for five days, and "every stratagem which French policy and Indian malice could invent was practiced to reduce the garrison."

Hoping to burn out the fort, the Indians set fire to the wooden fences that separated the fields. They also set fire to a log house about two hundred yards from the fort. In a very short time, the entire stockade was surrounded by fire, which was accompanied by hideous shouting and screaming by both the French and the Indians. Fire arrows were shot off, and several parts of the roof started to burn.

Inside the fort, while many of the soldiers continued to shoot, others dug trenches at the bottom of the stockade and passed buckets of water from hand to hand to extinguish the flames. They were able to wet all of the outside of the fort, and they kept it wet throughout five nights.

When the attackers saw that their fire arrows couldn't burn out the fort, they filled an abandoned farm cart with kindling and twigs, set it on fire and began rolling it toward the palisade. But even that did not work. Finally, General Dabeline promised that if Stevens would surrender the fort, his men could march out unharmed.

Captain Stevens knew that he had been sent to protect the fort, not surrender it, and he was suspicious of Dabeline's offer. He didn't trust either the French or their Indian conspirators. Stevens allowed his men to decide whether or not to give up. Each one voted to stand as long as possible. The captain reported their decision to General Dabeline, and the firing continued until the next morning. On the fifth day, the flag of truce was brought to the fort by two Indians. The Indians bargained that they would spare the fort if Stevens would sell provisions to Dabeline, but the captain drew a harder bargain. He told them he would not sell provisions for money. The French and Indians would get his food only if they would send him a captive for every five bushels of corn he gave them. The messengers retreated, four or five shots were fired, and the entire force withdrew.

For the next few months, Fort Number Four was quiet, and settlers began to return to their ruined farms. Within a short time, though, the fort was attacked again, as were other small isolated settlements in the Connecticut River valley. Settlers, frightened away for a short time, continued to return, however. By 1752, the colony became much more peaceful, and Benning Wentworth made the first of his famous grants in western New Hampshire. In 1752, Forts Number One, Two and Three were officially chartered as towns—and were given the names of Chesterfield, Westmoreland and Walpole. In 1753 Wentworth chartered Fort Number Four, which was called Charlestown. It seemed that the Connecticut River valley was finally ready to settle down into permanent, peaceful and prosperous communities.

9

The Years of the French and Indian War

Unfortunately, the brave settlers of the Connecticut River valley were in for more hardships a little sooner than they had expected. In 1754, the year after Charlestown was chartered, the French and Indian War began. This was the last and most intense of the series of Indian wars that had been going on for the previous seventy years. The first six years of the French and Indian War, from 1754 to 1760, were the hardest for the settlers at Charlestown.

Charlestown lay right in the line of march of the colonial troops who paced back and forth from Lake Champlain, and the town looked more like a military camp than a peaceful farming community. The war broke out sharply in the area when a band of Indians stealthily entered the town just after daylight and burst into the home of Captain James Johnson.

The Johnson farm was the most northerly outpost of the Charlestown community. The house was a big, sturdy log structure, in which Captain Johnson and his wife, Susanna, lived with their three children, Mrs. Johnson's sister, a maid and two hired men. It was about five hundred yards north of the fort, and its nearest neighbor was a blockhouse in the meadows.

The night before the attack, several neighbors had spent the evening "very cheerfully" at the Johnsons', eating watermelons and drinking flip, a drink made of eggs, rum, ale and spices. The Johnsons slept well until sunrise, when they heard a loud knock at the door. They thought it must be Peter Larrabee, a neighbor who was to do some carpentry for them that day. Captain Johnson opened the door and found himself surrounded by Indians.

The Indians broke into the house, dragged the family from their beds and led both adults and children to the door. The family was quickly bound and ordered to begin the dreadful march north toward Canada. The Indians knew that the Johnsons' neighbors had been alarmed and that soldiers were rapidly approaching. They panicked and began literally dragging the family northward through the thorny undergrowth.

The group continued for three miles without stopping. Finally, they sat down to a breakfast of bread, raisins and apples, all of which the Indians had looted from the house. The family had been sleeping at the time of the attack, and they had not even been given a chance to find shoes. The bare feet of Mrs. Johnson and her children had begun bleeding almost at once. They were now given rags to bind their feet, and Mrs. Johnson was placed on an old horse, which had also been stolen.

A day or so later along in the march, Mrs. Johnson gave birth to her fourth child, who was appropriately named Captive. She was then put back on the old horse to continue the journey. Eventually, however, food began to run low, and the horse was shot, roasted and eaten by the whole group.

For Mrs. Johnson and the baby, the Indians made a broth, "which was rendered almost a luxury by the seasoning of various roots." After many days of fording beaver ponds and forced marching through swamps and woods, the family arrived at East Bay on Lake Champlain. They were put in a canoe and taken into Canada, where they were separated, each going into a different family of Indians.

The Johnsons' life in captivity under the French extended for at least four years. Members of the family were imprisoned frequently, and they seldom had enough to eat. Eventually, Captain Johnson was given a parole to return to New England and obtain his family's ransom. Finally, Mrs. Johnson was released with Captive and another of her children. They went to Quebec, were able to board a ship that was crossing the Atlantic, and finally returned to the Connecticut Valley by way of London. Captain Johnson was released next, and the whole family was reunited in Charlestown in the fall of 1759.

Many other families suffered through similar adventures, but not all lived to see such happy endings. Yet, no matter how much hardship they had endured in captivity, many people returned as soon as possible to such isolated outposts as Fort Number Four and settled down quickly and quietly to resume their lives of farming and the building of a new nation.

While the pioneering western settlers were so bravely defending their homes, there were a number of men elsewhere in New Hampshire who were joining forces with citizens from the other New England colonies to wage an outright attack on the enemy.

In 1745, for example, four hundred New Hampshiremen, many of them as unskilled in military maneuvers as the farmers at Fort Number Four, were extremely successful when they joined Massachusetts troops to storm the French stronghold at Louisbourg. Louisbourg was a powerful for-

In 1745, four hundred New Hampshire soldiers helped capture the French stronghold at Louisbourg

tress known as the Gibraltar of the New World. It guarded the Atlantic approaches to the St. Lawrence River and Canada. On July 16, 1745, the Gibraltar of the New World fell. The New Hampshire troops captured the bell from the fort and brought it back to Portsmouth, where it still hangs in the belfry of St. John's Episcopal Church.

It later turned out that some New Hampshiremen had their own special brand of fighting ability. This ability proved to be tremendously valuable when the French and Indian War brought to a head the seemingly endless battles with the Indians. In 1756, a regiment from New Hampshire joined an expedition to Crown Point, the northern-

Captain Robert Rogers, shown in the company of several Indian braves

most and most important French stronghold on Lake Champlain.

These New Hampshire soldiers were such experts in scouting and in moving through deep woods that by the express desire of Lord Loudon, a high-ranking commander, they were formed into three companies of rangers. They were led by Captain Robert Rogers and were known as the Rogers Rangers. They continued to work through summer and winter and proved especially useful in intelligence work. They fought the Indians on their own terms through a series of successful skirmishes, were kept on throughout the war in the pay of the Crown and were retained on half pay when the war was over.

In 1759, the French fort at Niagara surrendered, and General James Wolfe claimed Quebec for the British. At this time, British forces appeared so far superior to the French that the British decided to take revenge on the Indians for their earlier devastation of the unprotected frontier. Captain Rogers was sent from Crown Point, accompanied by two hundred rangers. For twenty-one exhausting days, they marched until they came to the village of St. Francis. Rogers and two of his officers then entered the village in disguise. They found the Indians in the middle of a great war dance. Rogers returned to his men, formed them into parties and made a general attack just before daybreak.

The Indians were so surprised that they were totally unprepared to fight back. Some were killed in their homes, others were shot or tomahawked by parties stationed at the edges of the village. The village was almost completely wiped out. Rogers and a number of troops then marched along the St. Francis River, intending to meet another party of men at Upper Coos on the Connecticut River. The company, however, was pursued by other Indians and forced to scatter. Some found their way to Fort Number Four and others were lost in the woods.

Now that Quebec had been captured, it was time for the British to attack Montreal, a project in which many New Hampshiremen eagerly participated. In 1760, eight hundred men, under the command of Colonel John Goffe, marched to Fort Number Four, then cut a road directly through the woods to Crown Point. Then, under the command of Colonel Haviland, they went down Lake Champlain and on September 8, after several more French forts had fallen, Montreal surrendered.

War with the French and the Indians was over, after nearly a century of intermittent fighting, during which not one generation of New Hampshiremen had lived without fear of Indian attack.

10

The Fight
for Independence

The peace that followed the French and Indian War did not last long. Although the treaty of 1763 did bring an end to Indian raids, a new enemy was rising on the eastern horizon—the British.

Throughout the colonial period, the New Hampshire colonists had felt an increasing need to protect their own independence and freedom. Various acts of the British Parliament regulated trade with the mother country and with the other colonies and caused growing resentment among the merchants and citizens of the seacoast area.

Unlike many other North American colonies, New Hampshire was fortunate in having two native-born governors during the difficult period between 1741 and the Revolutionary War. The first of these, Benning Wentworth, guided his province through the difficult French and Indian War, and when he resigned in 1767, he handed over the governorship to his able nephew, John. Both governors were locally popular, and although Benning Wentworth's land-grant policies caused some trouble between New Hampshire and New York, both Wentworth administrations were times of internal political harmony.

As the relationship between Britain and her American colonies became more and more strained during the 1760s, the Wentworths tried to keep New Hampshire calm. However, King George was very much aware of the broad power of Benning Wentworth, and the governor was a little too popular for the king's liking. In 1763, a royal proclamation threatened Wentworth's removal. He was accused of failing to keep the king properly informed about his activities, and of granting lands too informally and carelessly. A resolution to remove Wentworth was actually adopted by the British ministry, but at the same time, agitation against British trade restrictions on the colonies was stirring up so much trouble that this resolution was lost in the turmoil of 1765.

Beginning in 1764, Parliament passed many acts that greatly limited trade between the American colonies and the West Indian islands. All of these acts together created an atmosphere of great uneasiness, suspicion and general unrest. Most upsetting to the colonists was the Stamp Act of 1765. By declaring that no legal document would be considered binding without the purchase of a special stamp, the British government hoped to make a large amount of money. Stamp Act commissioners were appointed to distribute the stamps throughout the American colonies.

The colonists felt that the Stamp Act practically bound them into slavery. The Virginia assembly passed a resolve in 1765 asserting the rights of the colonists, and the assembly of Massachusetts proposed a congress of deputies from each colony, who would try to decide on the best way in which the colonies might protect themselves.

A man named George Meserve was the commissioner assigned to distribute the stamps in New Hampshire.

Meserve was in England at the time of his appointment, and when he arrived in Boston, he was surprised to learn how deeply opposed the colonies were to the Stamp Act. He immediately saw that they had good reason for their concern, and he submitted his resignation to the authorities even before leaving Boston.

When Meserve arrived in Portsmouth, he found large dummies made in his likeness hanging from makeshift gallows all over town. He resigned again verbally before making any attempt to go to his own home, and his resignation was accepted with congratulations. So when the stamps arrived in Boston, there was no one to distribute New Hampshire's share.

Before the Stamp Act went into effect on November 1, the First Stamp Act Congress met in New York. Although no delegate from New Hampshire attended this meeting, the New Hampshire assembly adopted the measures that were agreed upon at the congress and sent petitions to England, as well as to the governor.

On October 31, the *New-Hampshire Gazette* appeared with a black mourning border that symbolized the way the citizens of Portsmouth felt about the stamps. Since no distributor had been found to replace Meserve, however, there weren't even any stamps in New Hampshire. The next day, though, the protest continued. Bells tolled, and a funeral procession was held for a dummy representing the Goddess of Liberty. When the "Goddess" was deposited in her grave, signs of life were supposedly discovered, and "Liberty" was carried off in triumph.

Public spirits were kept up by symbolic actions like these, and the repeal of the Stamp Act in March, 1766,

On October 31, 1765, the New-Hampshire Gazette *appeared with a black mourning band to show the colonists' hatred for the British Stamp Act*

☞ This is the Day before the never-to-be-forgotten STAMP-ACT was to take Place in *America*.

New-Hampshire Gᴇ ʀ GAZETTE,
AND
HISTORICAL CHRONICLE,

Thurſday October 3ᵗ, 1765. No. 474 { Weeks ſince thisPaper was firſt Publiſh'd.

—But what avail her unexhouſted Stores,
Her blooming Mountains and her ſunny Shores,
With all the Gifts that Heav'n and Earth impart,
The Smiles of Nature and the Charms of Art,
Which ſpread Oppreſſions in her Vallies Reigns,
And Tyranny uſurps her happy Plains?

WE are now arrived at the Eve of that remarkable Day, which is appointed to be as fatal to almoſt all that is dear to us, as the *Ides* of *March* were, to the Life of *Cæſar*, or as the memorable *Fifth* of *November* had like to have prov'd to the Lives, Liberty and Property of the honeſt People of *England*.—A Day on which our Slavery is to commence, by a Decree more ſevere, conſidering all Circumſtances, than was ever pronounced in the famous *Star-Chamber* ; an Ordinance by which we are not only to be reduced to Beggary by a TAX we can never pay, but are made Slaves for our Diſability, and are to be plunged into a deeper Bondage, by diſcharging of it, if it were in our Power.

And all this is determined by thoſe from whom by our Connection and Relation, we had the greateſt Reaſon to expect Defence, Protection and all the Favours and Bleſſings, that a dutiful Child cou'd expect, from a kind, tender Parent. For among other juſt Grounds for ſuch Hopes, *their* Predeceſſors for Ages paſt, eſteem'd it their Glory, as it was their Delight, to diffuſe Happineſs among all to whom their Influence extended. And more eſpecially to tranſmit to their Succeſſors Poſterity and Dependants, that *Liberty* which they themſelves enjoy'd, and thought worth defending and preſerving at any Rate. A very ſlighty Acquaintance with *Engliſh* Hiſtory, will inform any one, Ignorant of it, with what mighty Struggles and earneſt Contention, they have maintained this natural Right, againſt the united Force of Tyrants in various Forms, and all their Sycophants and adulating Adherents. And that they cou'd never be prevail'd upon, by all the Hopes and Allurements deſpotic Power and arbitrary Miſrule cou'd furniſh, or the World give in Exchange, to part with their own Freedom or intail Vaſſalage on their Poſterity : As without Liberty they juſtly thought all the Enjoyments of Life to a generous Mind, a Perſon freeborn, wou'd be inſipid, vapid and taſtleſs.

Oh *Liberty*, thou Goddeſs heav'nly bright,
Profuſe of Bliſs, and pregnant with Delight !
Eternal Pleaſures in thy Preſence reign,
And ſmiling Plenty leads thy wanton Train ;
Eas'd of her Load Subjection grows more light,
And Poverty looks chearful in thy Sight ;
Thou mak'ſt the gloomy Face of Nature gay,
Giv'ſt Beauty to the Sun & Pleaſure to the Day.

Thee Goddeſs, thee Britannia's Iſle adores :
How has ſhe oft exhauſted all her Stores,
How oft in Fields of Death thy Preſence ſought,
Nor thinks the mighty Prize too dearly bought.

Theſe, and ſuch as theſe, were the Sentiments of thoſe in Power, in former Times. They knew that Liberty, was the natural Right of Mankind : And that it was the greateſt Injury even to curtail or deprive them of it, in any Degree, any further than by their own Conſent they exchange Part of it, for other Bleſſings, and the Preſervation of what remains. They were ſo far from a Diſpoſition to rob Men of this natural Right, that on the contrary they were for enlarging, and extending of it to all the World that wou'd receive it. *Sed Tempora Mutantur &c.*—who that has read, that ſtrong metaphorical Exclamation, How is the Gold become dim, and the moſt fine Gold Changed ! can avoid thinking of it—it ſeems to obtrude itſelf on this Occaſion.—

What an amazing Change of Principles, Policy and Tempers !—One wou'd think a prodigious Vertigo had ſeiz'd every Head, that in the impetuous Whirl all Objects appeared alike— that there cou'd be no diſtinguiſhing Mercy from Cruelty, Right from Wrong.—Formerly every honeſt induſtrious Man was encouraged, his Diligence gained him Reputation as well as Subſiſtence. Can it be pretended the Caſe is the ſame, when no Man may buy or ſell but he that receives a Mark ?— a Badge of his Slavery, an Evidence of the Limitation of Property and the Loſs of Liberty.—Iſ honeſt Induſtry encouraged, when the moſt Induſtrious pay the more for excelling, and are ſubjected more than others to the imperious Mandates, probably of inſulting ſtrutting overbearing Officers ?

Was there any Thing more grievous and enſlaving in the Scheme to introduce a general Exciſe, propos'd about thirty Years ago to the People in G—— B——, than *This* is to us ?— and the Prime M——r of that Time who bro't in ſuch a Bill, it was ſaid cou'd have carried it through, (ſuch is the magic Power attending a certain high Office) yet what was the Event ? the general Diſguſt it gave, the Oppoſition to it, the People diſcover'd without Doors put anEnd to the Project.—And had it paſt into an Act, as was deſign'd, it wou'd never have been executed, but at the Head of a ſtanding Army.—As odious and deteſtable as this Scheme was, there were notwithſtanding a great many Advocates for it, prompted by the *Primum Mobile*.—And ſhould an Edict like that once paſt by the King of *Egypt*, relative to Male Children be promoted in the ſame Manner, there would no doubt be found a Majority for it within certain Walls, if it related only to the Colonies.—And indeed with reſpect to the preſentGeneration, ſuch an Edict wou'd not be ſo ſevere as theEdict now againſt us.—And ſhall we calmly and quietly yield our Necks to the Yoke ?— We have been told by ſome mercenary Scriblers, that the Right of paſſing ſuch a Law cannot be diſputed, that our Remedy is by humble Supplication,&c. and by this Way of Reaſoning one may prove that whatever is done by ſuperior Force is right, and to Robbery of any kind may be prov'd to be right, becauſe there was Power to perform the Action—and as to Petitioning and Remonſtrating,—What became of the humble Petitions preſented, while this Matter was under Conſideration,were they not ſpurn'd and frown'd as it were into Vaults.—They that repreſent us ought to hear us by their ownPrinciples—but the ſame firſt Mover remaining, we have Reaſon to think no Remonſtrances will ever be heard, no Reaſons prevail for our Relief in that Way.— Our own Reſolutions not to hold our Foreheads ſtill to receive the *Mark*, that is, not to be active to purchaſe our own Bondage from private ſelfiſh Views for fear of looſing a particular Intereſt, is the moſt probable Means of having the Difficulty removed, — and can any Thing follow from that worſe than will follow from Compliance ?—Will not this ſubject us to the ſameCondition of the Subjects of the *Grand Monarch*.—Will not he who ſeeks to ſave a petty Intereſt by ſuch Meaſures, become a Slave by his own Conſent ?—Does he not in effect agree to give up his Birth-Right, for a *Meſs of Pottage* ?—As thoſe who were to have been the Diſtributors of our Chains have generally diſdained ſuch an invidious Office, he will well deſerve Chains and every other *Mark of Slavery* who ſhall hunt after the *Mark of the Beaſt*, or fiſh as it were after *Sharks* ?—Let any one conſider what Character he is like to acquire who ſhould ſneak in private after what he will be aſhamed openly to avow. Who to ſave a paltry inſignificant Property, voluntarily

laid down his Neck and took on the Yoke of a perpetual Bondage, at a Time when his Townſmen, his Countrymen, and a whole Continent reſiſted and ſav'd themſelves from Ruin, the Loſs of Liberty and Property. Can there be any Doubt whether it is lawful? Let him that doubts, conſider, whether it is lawful for any Numbers of Men to ſell another Number as free as themſelves for Slaves ? Let them prove that theSale of *Joſeph* into *Egypt*, was lawful, and then they may doubt on—Let them determine whether, if a Magiſtrate, whoſeAuthority they acknowledge within his Juriſdiction, ſhou'd, becauſe he has aſſiſtance, order them where they were liable to a Moderate Fine, to be pilloried, whipt, and finally impriſoned for Life,they ſhou'd think themſelves obliged paſſively to ſubmit: If they do, let ſuch Friends to *Paſſive Obedience*,ſuffer the juſt Conſequence of their own Principles, till they receive Conviction.

The LAMENTATION
Of the
NEW-HAMPSHIRE-GAZETTE,
in particular, and the PRESS in general,
On a *Suſpicion* of loſing their LIBERTY.

—Cari ſunt nobis propinqui, familiares et amici,
ſed omnes omnium caritates, patria una eſt complexa,
pro qua quis bonus dubitet Mortem oppetere? ſi ſit
profuturus, et res ita requiret. Cicero.

BEHOLD THE GREAT, THE IMPORTANT DAY,
BIG with the FATE of CATO, and of ROME.
Addiſon.

WHAT a hard Caſe is it, that after this Day's Appearance upon the Stage of Action, *I muſt Die*, or ſubmit to that which is *worſe* than Death, be Stamp'd, and loſe my Freedom—Will all the goodDeeds I have done ſignify nothing ?—If the whole Kingdom of England would ſave my Life, I am unable to live *under* this Burden ; therefore I muſt *Die* !—O unhappy that I am—It is true, Life, like the Harmony in Muſic, is compoſed of the Contrarieties of ſeveral Notes, ſweet and harſh, ſharp and flat, ſprightly and ſolemn ; 'tis chequer'd with variety ofCircumſtances ; ſometimes it ſwells with a proſperous Fortune ; at others it ebbs into the loweſt Degree of Adverſity ; and ſeldom admits of Conſtancy and Durability— It is true, my Life in theſe Parts have been *but ſhort*, having this Day compleated *nine Years and five Weeks*— FREEDOM is ſo natural, and SLAVERY ſo contrary to my Nature, that I chuſe a *voluntary* Death, in Hopes of eſcaping this Servitude—Should I once ſubmit to have my Liberty infring'd, I could never make that Appearance in the World I have, therefore as honorable Death is to be prefer'd before an *ignominious* Life —I was reſolv'd to live well ; and be as uſeful as I could, without being concern'd as to the *Length* or *Shortneſs* of my Duration— But before I make my *Exit*, I will recount over ſome of the many good Deeds I have done, and how uſeful I have been, and ſtill may be, provided my Life ſhould be ſpar'd ; or I might hereafter revive again, altho' it may not ſeem ſo proper to ſound my ownPraiſe. Without this Art of communicating to the Public, how dull and melancholy muſt all the intelligent Part of Mankind appear ?—It may with great Veracity beaffirm'd,that there is no Art, Science or Profeſſion in theWorld,but what owes its Origin, ar at leaſt its Progreſs and preſen brought great rejoicing to the American colonies. But on the very same day, the Declaratory Act was passed. This act stated that Parliament had full authority to make laws binding the American colonies "in all cases whatsoever." The Portsmouth town meeting was held, and an urgent plea was made to the colonial assembly to petition against the new Act. The assembly in turn urged that a boycott of English goods be enforced.

Into this teeming whirlpool of political unrest stepped John Wentworth to assume the responsibilities of governor. In 1767, when Wentworth took over the post from his uncle, he probably never suspected that he was to be New Hampshire's last royal governor. His major interest was in the colony, and he cultivated the good will of his people. Although he had been brought up to be a merchant, he had a great interest in agriculture, and he wanted to develop unsettled areas of the province. He spent much time traveling through the wooded regions north and west of Portsmouth, exploring the land and planning new roads.

The governor's interest in improving the colony received a great deal of attention and recognition, and to some extent it distracted the New Hampshire people from the general political difficulties with England. John Wentworth was so popular that the Townshend Act, passed in 1767, received little attention in New Hampshire. In this Act, Parliament laid duties on tea, paper, lead, glass and painters' colors. While other colonies agreed not to import these products, Wentworth's popularity and the influence of his rich friends and relatives prevented such an agreement from being adopted in New Hampshire.

In 1770, another similar act was passed, but the united boycott of the other colonies on taxable British goods caused British manufacturers to lose a great deal of money. The British merchants, therefore, influenced Parliament to repeal the Townshend Acts at about the same time the newspapers such as the *New Hampshire Gazette* were calling for the people to rise up in arms.

Up until the early 1770s the governor had managed to keep his popularity, but he was, after all, a royal governor, and he felt that he had to support the British government. This made it extremely difficult for him to deal with the anti-British sentiments at home—especially when these sentiments were converted into actions.

Early in 1774, matters between New Hampshire and England came to a head. Parliament insisted on its right to tax American imports of tea. The colonists responded by refusing to import the tea, and made use of the only peaceful means available to them to oppose Britain's "right" to tax —a boycott. The boycott succeeded, and the warehouses of the East India Company were soon filled with an unsaleable supply of tea. Parliament then withdrew the tax and stated that the East India Company might ship tea directly to America—but subject to a duty of three shillings a pound.

This duty, many colonists felt, was just as outrageous as the tax had been. Trading towns set an example by refusing to permit East India Company tea to be either landed or sold. In New Hampshire, though, a cargo of twenty-seven chests of tea was landed and placed in the customs house before the people could prevent it. A town meeting was quickly called to decide what to do about the situation. The voters agreed to propose that Mr. Perry, the man to whom the tea had been sent, reship the tea. He consented, and a guard was appointed to see that no damage was done. Since the tea had already been brought into the colony, the duty had to be paid, and Mr. Perry paid it. Governor Wentworth convened his council to make sure no violence would occur, and the tea was peacefully reshipped to Halifax.

Before long, though, a second cargo of thirty chests of tea arrived, also addressed to Mr. Perry. There was a small disturbance, and the windows of Perry's home were shattered.

Brigadier General John Sullivan led the assault on Fort William and Mary

He applied to the governor for protection, but the towns-people, through their committee, insisted that he ship the tea to Halifax. The duty was paid, and again, the tea was shipped off without violence.

Massachusetts, however, was not able to resolve its tea crisis so peacefully—as the famous Boston Tea Party demonstrated. The port had to be closed, and guarded by warships. A military governor was brought to Boston, and he began to gather British troops. The other colonies were in sympathy with Massachusetts, and a union seemed absolutely essential.

So the first Continental Congress was called. It was held in Philadelphia, beginning on September 5, 1774. Twelve colonies sent fifty-six delegates, among them John Sullivan and Nathaniel Folsom of New Hampshire. The New Hampshire assembly, which had met in July in a special session to appoint these delegates, also recommended that New Hampshiremen assist their distressed brethren in Massachusetts, and contributions were raised in many towns.

In the fall of 1774, Governor Wentworth began to strengthen the garrison at Fort William and Mary, in accordance with a royal order to seize all arms and ammunition in the colonies. British merchants were now forbidden to export gunpowder and other military stores to America. The Committee of Safety in Portsmouth, warned by Paul Revere of a proposed British attempt to remove the New Hampshire powder to Boston, decided to attempt an attack on the fort to get all the supplies they could. On December 14, 1774, four hundred men marched on Fort William and Mary. The captain of the fort and his five men were held, and one hundred barrels of powder were carried off.

On December 15, another company removed fifteen of the light cannon and all the side arms. These were then hidden in the various seacoast towns, under the care of the Committees of Safety. This second storming of the fort was undertaken just before the frigate *Scarborough* and the sloop *Canseau* arrived, containing several companies of British soldiers. These soldiers quickly took possession of the fort and of those heavy cannon that the colonists had not been able to carry off.

The governor wanted to prosecute the leaders of the raid for high treason. He issued a proclamation commanding all civil and military officers to assist in finding and capturing the men who stole the cannon from the fort. At the same time, an association was formed by the governor and some of his friends to promote support of the royal government. They boasted that a hundred men from the *Scarborough* and the *Canseau* were just waiting for a moment's notice to assist the governor in maintaining royal law and order.

On January 25, 1775, a convention met in Exeter to appoint delegates to the next general congress. The convention also issued an address to the people, warning them of the danger of remaining under British rule and urging them to unite to defend the countryside from invasion.

Soon after this convention, New Hampshiremen began to think seriously about how they would go about defending their liberty. There were old laws that stated that every male between sixteen and sixty had to be provided with a musket and bayonet, a knapsack, a cartridge box, one pound of bullets and twelve flints. The law also provided that every town had to have on hand a barrel of powder, two hundred pounds of lead and three hundred flints, for every sixty men. In peacetime, these regulations were often ignored, but, fortunately for the colonists, only a few years earlier the governor had taken care to appoint officers and militia, and review the regiments.

In early 1775 each town had a Committee of Safety, and these committees were also Committees of Correspondence, which meant that all intelligence information about the actions of the British was passed from committee to committee, from town to town. When the committees learned that General Thomas Gage was prepared to open active warfare, twelve hundred men marched out of New Hampshire to assist their brothers in Boston. Some of these men returned home, but others formed themselves into two regiments ready for action at any time.

On May 17, 1775, the New Hampshire assembly voted to raise two thousand men, in three regiments. The men agreed to serve until the last day of December, 1775, unless they were discharged sooner.

The very presence of the *Scarborough* in Portsmouth Harbor created tension in New Hampshire. The actions of her crew were particularly offensive. All vessels heading for the harbor were seized by the British and sent to Boston. Fishermen on New Castle Island were prevented from going out to catch fish. On the other hand, New Hampshiremen kept the *Scarborough*'s crew from buying provisions from the town and harassed the British ship in other ways. A compromise was finally reached, though. Fishing boats were allowed to go out, and the British were allowed to buy their provisions in Portsmouth.

Meanwhile, on June 13, a group of Portsmouth residents surrounded the house of John Wentworth and demanded the surrender of the governor's royalist guest, John Fenton. When Fenton refused to give himself up, the citizens set up a cannon in front of the house and threatened to destroy the house and everyone in it. Later that night, Governor Wentworth, his wife, Frances, and their newborn son, Charles-Mary, fled to Fort William and Mary, never to return to Portsmouth.

The flight of John Wentworth marked the end of almost a century and a half of royal government in New Hampshire. Wentworth's personal popularity had been enough to sustain him throughout the early years of discontent with the British, but the people's knowledge of his loyalty to the Crown, and his personal needs to fulfill the Crown's demands, brought about his downfall.

A week after Wentworth's departure, twelve hundred New Hampshiremen marched to Bunker Hill, and New Hampshire citizens were certain that colonial rule had come to an end. With the meeting of New Hampshire's Continental Congress in Exeter on May 17, 1775, New Hampshire plunged into the Revolutionary War. Then regiments were established on May 20, and West Hampshiremen took part in the Battle of Bunker Hill on June 17. By the time Thomas Jefferson drafted his Declaration of Independence which was adopted on July 4, 1776, New Hampshire was already well on the way to its fight for independence.

While Bunker Hill was only the beginning of a long, bloody and difficult fight, New Hampshire had dramatically demonstrated to herself and her neighbors that New Hampshiremen were unwilling to be colonials any longer. Times might be hard for the remainder of the Revolutionary period, but every New Hampshire farmer knew that no foreign government would ever again be able to tax him unfairly, and that one day, before long, he would finally be able to sow his corn and raise his cattle in peace.

In CONGRESS, July 4, 1776.

The unanimous Declaration of the thirteen united States of America.

*Josiah Bartlett, William Whipple and Matthew Thornton signed
the Declaration of Independence in the last column*

Bibliography

FASSETT, JAMES H. *Colonial Life in New Hampshire.* Boston: Ginn & Co., 1899. Athenaeum Press.

PRICE, BERTHA WESTON. *Legends of Our Lakes and Rivers.* Lennoxville, Quebec, Canada: Bertha Weston Price, 1937.

SPEARE, EVA C. *Indians of New Hampshire.* Littleton, N.H.: Courier Press, 1965.

————*New Hampshire Folk Tales.* Littleton, N.H.: Courier Press, 1964.

WINSLOW, OLA E. *Portsmouth.* New York. Macmillan, 1966.

For advanced readers and teachers:

BELKNAP, JEREMY. *History of New Hampshire.* Boston: Isaiah Thomas and Ebenezer T. Andrews, 1791.

BREWSTER, CHARLES W. *Rambles About Portsmouth.* Portsmouth: Lewis W. Brewster, Portsmouth Journal Office, 1859.

SQUIRE, JAMES DUANE. *The Granite State.* New York: American Historical Company Inc., 1956.

Historical New Hampshire, a magazine issued quarterly by the New Hampshire Historical Society since 1944, contains many articles and illustrations pertaining to the Colonial period.

Important Dates

1000—Irish or Norse attempt colony at North Salem.

1603—Martin Pring arrives in the *Speedwell*.

1605—Samuel de Champlain explores the New Hampshire coast for France.

1613—John Smith visits the Isles of Shoals.

1622—David Thomson settles at Odiorne's Point.

1623—Dover is settled.

1629—Laconia Company is formed.
  —Edward Hilton receives his patent.

1631—Portsmouth is chartered.

1633—First Church in New Hampshire is organized at Dover.

1634—First masts shipped from New Hampshire for Royal Navy.

1638—Exeter is settled by John Wheelwright.
  —Winicunet settled.

1640—Dover settlers make "Dover Combination."

1673—Dunstable is chartered by Massachusetts General Court.

1679—New Hampshire becomes Royal Province.
  —King James appoints James Cutt president of the colony.

1682—Militia is established.

1686—New Hampshire enters Dominion of New England.

1690—New Hampshire and Massachusetts are reunited.

1692—Union between New Hampshire and Massachusetts is dissolved, Samuel Allen becomes governor.

1697—Hannah Dustin is captured.

1741–67—Benning Wentworth is governor.

1745—Expedition against Louisbourg.

1749—Benning Wentworth makes first grant west of Connecticut River.

1754—French and Indian War begins.

1755—Rogers Rangers are organized.

1763—Treaty of Paris ends French and Indian War.

1765—Stamp Act is passed by the British.

1767—John Wentworth becomes governor.

1769—Dartmouth College is chartered.

1771—First class is graduated from Dartmouth College.

1774—First Continental Congress meets in Philadelphia on September 5.

—Fort William and Mary is seized by Patriots on December 14.

1775—Governor Wentworth flees Portsmouth on June 13.

—Battle of Bunker Hill on June 17.

1776—Declaration of Independence proclaimed on July 4.

—Declaration of Independence signed August 2.

Places to Visit

Readers may wish to visit the following sites of historical interest in New Hampshire.

CONCORD. New Hampshire Historical Society, 30 Park Street. A library and museum are maintained in the Society building, which is open Monday through Saturday from 9 A.M to 4 P.M. Permanent exhibits include four period rooms, housing the Prentis Collection of New England furnishings, 1680–1730.

DOVER. Woodman Institute, 182 Central Avenue. Open the year round from 2 to 5 P.M., except Monday. Exhibits include birds, animals, insects, reptiles, minerals, Indian artifacts and weapons. The seventeenth-century Damm Garrison House is preserved here.

EXETER. Gilman Garrison House, 12 Water Street. Built about 1650, remodeled in eighteenth century. Log structure of original garrison contains furnishings of both periods.

FRANKLIN. Daniel Webster Birthplace, just off Route 127 between Franklin and Salisbury. Built around 1780, this is the boyhood home of Daniel Webster orator, congressman and twice Secretary of State.

HILLSBORO. Franklin Pierce Homestead. A National Historic Landmark, this has been completely restored to reflect the 1804–39 period when the younger Pierce lived at home before starting his career.

PORTSMOUTH. Governor John Langdon Mansion Memorial, 143 Pleasant Street. Built in 1784, described by Washington as the "handsomest house in Portsmouth." Open: June, September to mid-October, weekdays 1 to 5 P.M.

The Moffat-Ladd House, 154 Market Street. Built 1763. Home of General Williams Whipple, signer of the Declaration of Independence. Eighteenth-century mansion, counting house and garden. Open: May 15 to October.

Richard Jackson House, Northwest Street. Built in 1664. Open: mid-June to mid-September.

Strawbery Banke, ten acres of site of 1630 settlement of Portsmouth, originally named Strawbery Banke, with thirty seventeenth-, eighteenth- and nineteenth-century houses being preserved. Open: weekdays, 10 A.M. to 5 P.M., Sundays, 12 to 5 P.M.

Warner House, Daniel and Chapel Streets (circa 1716). An engaging glimpse of how people of importance lived in eighteenth-century Portsmouth. Open: mid-May to mid-October 10 to 5 P.M. on weekdays. 2 to 5 P.M. on Sundays.

Wentworth-Coolidge Mansion. Two miles from Portsmouth proper. Original home of Benning Wentworth, New Hampshire's first Royal Governor (1741–67).

Times and admission prices may change without notice.

Index

Masonian Proprietors, 63
Massachusetts Bay Colony, 50, 51, 52, 53, 54, 58
Massachusetts General Court, 24, 51, 54
Massachusetts Puritans, 52
Massachusetts Rule, 52
Masts, 45, 46
Mast Roads, 46
Mast Ships, 47
Mathews, 25
Meetinghouses, 22, 25
Merrimack River, 4, 9, 10, 16, 20, 50, 53, 54, 70, 72
Meserve, George, 83, 84
Middlesex County, 54
Moore, 25
Mount Washington, 19

Nashua, 54
Neal, 25
Neale, Captain Walter, 19, 20, 51
Needham, Nicholas, 26
Neff, Mary, 15
Newburyport, 61
Newington, 36
New Castle (Delaware), 42, 70
New Castle Island, 91
New England, 5
New Hampshire
 as a part of Massachusetts, 28
 beauty of, 18
 churches, 35, 65
 Colonial Wars, 39, 65, 66, 68, 69, 70, 76, 81, 82
 explorers, 2, 3, 4, 5, 9, 10, 11, 19, 45
 exports, 33, 34, 42, 43, 44, 45, 46, 47, 48, 49, 62
 farming, 6, 32, 33, 34
 first graveyard, 7
 fishing, 6, 8, 28, 42, 43, 49
 food, 30, 31, 32, 33, 34
 government, 2, 5, 7, 26, 55, 56, 57, 58, 59
 homelife, 30
 homes, 1, 29, 30
 imports, 43, 44
 industry, 34, 35, 40, 44, 45, 46, 47, 49, 61
 lakes, 19
 linen, 34, 35
 livestock, 34
 massacres, 15
 meetinghouses, 34, 35, 36
 military protection, 58
 military requirements, 90

ministers, 22, 25
 natural resources, 6, 7, 18, 19, 23, 27, 28, 29
 religion, 51, 52, 53, 65
 rivers, 10, 20, 21, 37, 53
 sawmills, 46
 schools, 36, 37, 38, 55, 65
 settlements, 4, 23
 taverns, 39–40
 tools, 32, 34, 35
 trade, 19, 44, 45, 49, 51, 61
New Hampshire Assembly, 57
New Hampshire Continental Congress, 91
New Hampshire Gazette, 84, 87
Newmarket, 43
Nickerson, Colonel, 16
Norridgewock Indians, 72
Norse, 1
Northam, 21
North Salem, 1, 2
Norton, 25
Nutter, Anthony, 56

Odiorne's Point, 5, 52 (*See also* Rye)
Ossipee Mountain Range, 19
Ossipees, 9
Oyster River, 69 (*See also* Durham)

Pannaway, 4, 6, 7, 20, 21, 23, 25, 29, 42, 45, 52
Pannaway House, 6, 7
Pannaway Plantation, 6, 7, 23, 42
Passaconaway, 12, 13
Pennacook, 9, 12, 13, 68
Pennacook Confederacy, 9, 13
Penobscot, 10
Penobscot Bay, 4
Pequawket, 9, 11, 12, 68
Perry, Mr., 87, 88
Phipps, Sir William, 69
Pied Cowe, 23, 25
Piscataway River, 3, 5, 6, 7, 10, 21, 23, 45, 47, 49, 53, 55
Plymouth Colony, 5, 7, 13, 29, 52
Portsmouth, 21, 23, 24, 25, 42, 43, 59, 63, 79, 84, 86, 91
Post riders, 39
Post route, 39
Presbyterians, 61
Presidential Mountain Range, 19
Pring, Martin, 2, 3, 9
Province of Laconia (*See* Laconia)

Quaker women, 53